Janell T.

Chains
in China

Chains
in China

Imprisoned for his faith, Pastor Chen suffered
incredible trials for God in communist China.

Bradley Booth

Pacific Press®
Publishing Association

Nampa, Idaho | Oshawa, Ontario, Canada
www.pacificpress.com

Cover design by Steve Lanto
Cover design resources from istockphoto.com
Inside design by Aaron Troia

You can obtain additional copies of this book by calling toll-free 1-800-765-6955 or by visiting http://www.adventistbookcenter.com.

Library of Congress Cataloging-in-Publication Data
Booth, Bradley, 1957- author.
    Chains in China : imprisoned for his faith, Pastor Chen suffered incredible trials for God in communist China / Bradley Booth.
        pages cm
    ISBN 13: 978-0-8163-5732-1 (pbk.)
    ISBN 10: 0-8163-5732-3 (pbk.)
    1. Chen, 1927- 2. Seventh-day Adventists—China—Clergy—Biography. I. Title.
    BX6193.C44B66 2015
    286.7092—dc23
    [B]
                                                                        2014042093

February 2015

Contents

Chapter 1

The warm, yellow sun was just coming up over the eastern horizon as Chen stepped out into the back streets of old Shanghai. Little finches chittered in the Chinese lantern bushes along the sidewalk, pausing only long enough to watch him as he passed. He bent his head to smell the blossoms of the hydrangea flowers climbing on the little trellis over the front gate. *What a gift from God,* he thought as he drank in the sweet fragrance of the snow-white blossoms.

But that was only the reality of the moment in Chen's eyes from the front door of his uncle's small bungalow. The real world outside this peaceful place he called home was one of war—world war.

Hitler's German machine had joined forces with Italy and Japan to conquer the world, and for a time, it looked like they were unstoppable. The Germans had invaded almost all of Europe, and even parts of Africa and the Soviet Union. Italy fought side by side with Germany in the Mediterranean, forcing the Allied armies to focus on North Africa instead of on Europe where the real war was raging.

The Japanese were a different story altogether, and they had one goal in mind—to dominate Asia and the Pacific completely. In the early thirties, they invaded Manchuria and went to war with China. Next, they got a stranglehold on the islands of the Pacific and much of Southeast Asia, including Burma, Thailand, and Hong Kong. Then, in 1941, the Japanese attacked Pearl Harbor, bringing the United States into the war. Fortunately, the Allied armies led by the British and the Americans slowed the Japanese down enough to gain an edge in Burma, southern China, and the Pacific Islands.

And when the Germans were finally beaten and called a truce on May 7, 1945, Japan was the only Axis nation left fighting to reach its war goals. They were badly crippled now, pushed back into the upper Pacific, and the small island of Japan was a mere shadow of the military monster that had raised its ugly head some ten years before. But the Japanese were fighting on, and it appeared they were determined to fight to the last man. World newspapers were all saying that if the Allied nations could not stop them, millions more might have to die in the continuing struggle.

What a mess this world war has become, Chen thought. Power-hungry men had started it for the sake of gaining territory by force, and they were willing to sacrifice countless lives in the process. Only God could fully know the devastation and horror these cruel despots had brought upon our world.

Chen continued down the dusty streets of Shanghai on his way to the business section of town. Until now, he had been working at a shoe factory making boots for soldiers in the army. That had been his job for three years running, since the day he had dropped out of school for good. He had not been old enough to be drafted into the military as a soldier to join the war against Japan—until now. Today he turned eighteen, the magic number that required him to enlist.

Not that he wanted to enlist. He hated the idea of war. War was so violent, cruel, and pathetically senseless! But that didn't mean he wouldn't have to go to war. Young men were more easily trained—a premium in wartime. He might never see action on a battlefield, but then again, he might. Having to carry a gun, master guerilla warfare, or man a tank was not his idea of fun.

But how could he escape his duty? He could just fail to show up at the enlistment stations, or falsify the papers that identified his age, or simply run away where no one could find him. But he knew those weren't real options. Sooner or later, someone would come looking for him, and when they did, it wouldn't be a pretty picture. He had to think long and hard about that one.

Besides, Chen was a Seventh-day Adventist and had been one all his life. Adventists were supposed to be loyal to their country and their God. The principles of the Bible did not allow Christians to become cowards, to run away and hide. Of course, there were always the issues of carrying a gun with intent to kill and Sabbath observance. In the military, he wouldn't have a choice about either one. When a soldier was enlisted, he was supposed to obey his commanding officer. Was Chen willing to carry a gun and use it to kill? That was an easy question for a non-Christian to answer, but for a Seventh-day Adventist, it was different. Chen knew he had been put on this earth to save lives, not take them.

And Sabbath observance? He knew he would never violate the holy Sabbath hours no matter what they did to him—even if they beat him, even if they put him in prison, even if they shot him with a firing squad. Chen didn't want to think about that option.

He just needed to sign up. And that's where he was headed right now—army headquarters. They probably wouldn't call him in for service anyway. There were millions of young men Chen's age. What were the chances he would be selected?

Chen made a beeline to the town's business district. His boss at the shoe factory had given him the morning off to find the enlistment office, fill out the proper papers, and get his identification.

Eighteen years of age. In Chen's mind, he was still just a boy. His father had told him stories about the Great War, or World War I, as everyone was calling it now. There had been so much senseless bloodshed in that war, and no one had really considered themselves winners. Not even the victors. Nearly two hundred billion dollars had been spent to reshape the countries of Europe and Asia, and as many as thirty-five million people had lost their lives. *What a waste of human life,* Chen thought. That was a lot of money in anyone's book, particularly in the 1940s when everyone was just coming out of a worldwide depression.

The men at the enlistment office were polite enough, though Chen had heard stories about what the army was really like once a soldier got drafted. "We'll send a letter notifying you when and where you must go to serve," the man behind the desk told Chen.

That night, when he got home, Chen's uncle Renshu handed him a letter. Chen's heart skipped a beat. The enlistment officer couldn't possibly be calling him this quickly, could he? He had just signed up today! There was no office address on the outside of the envelope, so he didn't know whom it was from. However, when he tore open the letter, he got the surprise of his life.

"Dear Chen," the letter began. "We would like to invite you to become a Bible worker for the Seventh-day Adventist Church in Shanghai. The job will require you to work long hours going door-to-door selling Bibles and other religious books. It will also require you to have a good knowledge of the Bible and be willing to give Bible studies to those who are interested. If this is something you would like to discuss, please contact Pastor Lin David at the Shanghai Seventh-day Adventist Church."

Chen didn't know what to say. He had often wondered what it would be like to work as a Bible worker but never thought he would be chosen for such a task. "Thank you so much for your kind offer," he wrote in a letter in response to Pastor Lin that very night. "I would very much like to become a Bible worker and am willing to begin when you need me. I think I must let you know, however, that I just turned eighteen and could be drafted into the army at any time. I am praying God will let me serve His church rather than the army but am willing to let God lead."

"Don't get your hopes up," his uncle told him as he watched Chen put his return letter into an envelope and address it. "If and when the army calls you, that is a summons you will have to obey. Remember, it is God's will that you obey the laws of our land too, unless, of course, these laws require you to break the commandments of our God."

"Yes, sir," was all Chen could say, but he was very worried now. What if he

9

was called to serve in the army after all, as his uncle had said? What if he had to go away to war? He would much rather fight in the Lord's army against the forces of darkness than fight in an army against the Japanese.

"Please, Lord," Chen prayed by his bedside that night. "This is a dream come true! Let me serve You as a Bible worker. There are lots of young men my age who would make good soldiers for China, but not many who would be willing to fight the kinds of battles I will be fighting for You with my Bible in hand."

The days ticked by. July came and went, and the sultry days of August soon arrived. Chen quit his job at the shoe factory making boots for soldiers and went to work as a Bible worker for the church in Shanghai. However, any day now he expected to hear from the army enlistment office.

And he watched the papers. News about the war was splashed all over the newspapers every night, and as he read the news articles, he had to wonder what would come next. However, the news he got on the evening of August 6 was not what he was expecting at all.

He was just walking down the steps to the Seventh-day Adventist Church when he saw people running and shouting in the streets. Many were waving newspapers in their hands, and he ran down among them to see what the commotion was all about. "Listen to this!" someone was shouting as he read the lead story, and the noise in the street died away as everyone stopped to listen.

"On August 6, 1945, at 8:15 A.M., the United States dropped an atomic bomb on Hiroshima, Japan, totally destroying the city. It is not known how many causalities resulted from the explosion, but the most recent census of Hiroshima lists the population at over eighty thousand. All reports tell us there were no survivors."

Chen leaned against a street lamp to steady himself. What an alarming, surprising turn of events! The Japanese had been dealt a terrible blow, and who could say what would happen now? Would they surrender? Did the Americans have more bombs like this one, and if so, would they drop them on Japan?

No one knew the answers, but three days later, on August 9, the Japanese city of Nagasaki was also bombed, sealing the fate of Japan. World War II would be over now, it was said. China was safe, and that meant Chen was safe. He wouldn't have to serve in the Chinese army to fight battles with guns and grenades. He could serve in the Lord's army instead, fighting the battles of the great controversy between good and evil. That was a war Chen knew he could win. God's church might lose a few battles in the process, but the war was already over the day Jesus died on the cross.

Thank You, Lord, was all he could say as he rode his bicycle home that evening. *God works in mysterious ways to answer our prayers,* Chen thought, but never in his wildest dreams had he expected God to do it in this way.

Chains in China

Chapter 2

Born in Ning Bo, China, in 1927 to Adventist parents, Chen had been raised to serve the church. His father's responsibilities as a missionary evangelist for the church in the Zhe Jiang province had always kept the family on the move. This made life difficult for the family in so many ways. When he was in the primary grades, Chen couldn't stay in a school for more than three or four months at a time because of his father's travels. His sporadic school attendance influenced his credits and grades, and kept him from going on to middle school. That was a real disadvantage, and in the years to come, he was to suffer the effects of it.

Unfortunately, his misadventures with schooling had pushed him into a life of work too early, which he resented. At the age of fifteen, he had left school for good and gone to Shanghai to become an apprenticed student laborer. All young men not in school did this at the time. To make matters worse, World War II was on, and everyone had to work overtime at the factory to keep up with the wartime government quotas.

Times had been difficult, and Chen worked as hard as anyone, but he knew he would not stay there forever. He was born for more than just factory work. God had something better for him, he was sure. And though he wasn't yet clear on what that something might be, he prayed that God would lead him in that fateful decision.

His parents had always wanted him to be a pastor like his father. He'd once heard his father talking to a friend about Chen being the firstborn and that Chen had been dedicated to the service of God as a child. This put a lot of pressure on Chen as a boy because he knew his parents expected him to do something special with his life for God.

Chen loved his father and mother, and he respected them for the sacrifices they had made for God and for the church. He wanted to please them. Family honor means everything in Chinese culture, but Chen had been wary, knowing what the future probably held for him as a pastor. He wasn't sure he could be the preacher his father was. He also wasn't sure he was ready for the responsibilities of being a pastor. And yet it seemed he had no voice in the matter, as was customary in the home of an Asian family. As his father had said so many times, his lot was the life of a pastor.

But now Chen had a new lease on life, a new job that let him learn and grow spiritually. He wasn't a preacher. He wasn't a church pastor. He was working as a Bible worker for the Seventh-day Adventist Church in Shanghai, and he loved it like nothing he had ever loved before. In this new job, he would be paid to study his Bible and share it with others, among other things. What an opportunity! What a blessing!

The weeks flew by, and before long, Chen was experiencing all kinds of new adventures. He was selling Bibles and other religious books the church could manage to get, and that was a blessing for everyone, helping the church grow. One hindrance to Chen's mission, however, was that books in the Chinese language were expensive, if you could find them at all. And the church had very few of the books they really needed by Ellen White from America. For Chen, her books were the most inspirational of all next to the Bible. After all, she had been inspired through visions and actual visits by angels. When Chen thought about that, it made his mind tingle, and he found himself wanting to devote his life to book and Bible work more than ever.

What they really needed was to find a way to translate some of the Ellen White books themselves. That way, they could cut the costs down and print many copies of the books independently. He mentioned this to Pastor Lin at the Shanghai church, and the pastor was impressed with such an idea.

But the thing Chen enjoyed doing most of all was studying the Bible with interested people. He usually found these people when he was out selling his Bibles and other religious books. If they could buy a book, that was good because it helped him make a living, but if they couldn't buy, he would often invite them to study with him. And if they enjoyed the studies, he would ask them if they wanted to visit the Seventh-day Adventist Church with him in Shanghai.

He did not make much money as a Bible worker, but that didn't matter to him much. He was young and unattached, and he needed little in the way of earthly possessions. While he had a bicycle to help him get around the city, he didn't even own a watch. That was the sum total of his earthly goods, except a few nice shirts that he had to wash and iron almost daily—but he figured that was good practice for when he might want to court a girl someday.

"A young woman likes to see her man all dressed up nice," his mother had told him more than once, and he guessed she was right. It certainly didn't hurt any, and being dressed up always helped him get into homes when he was selling books. That was a plus in itself.

Chains in China

After two years on the job, he was an excellent salesman, though he had to admit he probably gave away as many books as he sold. "How can I leave the people's homes without giving them something to read?" he asked Pastor Lin.

He was also a good Bible student and could find his way around the Bible as well as any pastor. He didn't know it at the time, but the work he was doing as a Bible worker in Shanghai undoubtedly prepared him better for his future life of service than anything else he would do. As long as he was sharing the gospel story about the love of Jesus, that's all that mattered to him. He didn't care where that might be or what trials God might ask him to go through. If God wanted him to climb the mountains of Everest, he would do it. If sharing the story of salvation required him to sail the seven seas, then that was where he wanted to be. Life for him was all about evangelism and adventure for Jesus at any price.

But there were other adventures coming for Chen, too, changes that would shape his future in ways he could not imagine. He could not always read the handwriting on the wall of his life; however, in the years to come, he would wish he had been wise enough to do so. His energy and enthusiasm were his greatest gifts, but he was young and naïve at times about life, and Satan would find ways to exploit that.

While in Shanghai doing the Lord's work, he met the woman of his dreams, and what a girl she was! Ruolan was like no girl Chen had ever met. She was exciting, funny, and so in love with life. Her name meant "orchid," a name Ruolan's father had insisted on giving her. "With a name like that, she will always be beautiful," he had said when she was just a baby, and Chen had to agree with him.

Chapter 3

Chen and Ruolan met in the home church where Chen worshiped each Sabbath. She had been invited by a friend and was intrigued by the community spirit she found there. The church was very caring toward the poor and sick, always ready to help those in distress, it seemed. When a church member in the community lost his job, another member would show up at his door with food or clothes. When people in the church group got sick, someone came to their house to treat them with herbs and other medicines.

And when Ruolan joined Chen's Bible study group at the church, she learned why the members were so kind and loving. It was because they were filled with the peace and love of God. Jesus had died for them to save them from a world filled with tragedy. If they prayed to Him, He would help them with their troubles. But most important to Ruolan was the incredible news that this God, called Jesus, was coming soon to take them all to heaven!

And so it was that Ruolan learned about the great Bible truths. She was young, bright-eyed, and intelligent, and she seemed to know exactly what she believed. She was excited about the ideas she was hearing and would share her joy about this newfound faith during personal testimony time. She didn't always understand everything she heard from the Bible, but she felt drawn to this message and these people who had brought her the good news of salvation.

Week by week, Chen found himself looking forward to Sabbath services. Week by week, he found himself more attracted to this woman who was bringing life to his church. They spent hours riding bikes together on the weekend, walking in the parks, and cooking their favorite dishes.

He could not know that he was treading upon dangerous ground. He could see the road but not the bend in the road, and it was this lack of foresight that was to be his downfall.

One thing that bothered Chen more than he wanted to admit was the lack of missionary focus in Ruolan's life. She seemed to love the message of hope the Adventist Church had brought her, but she felt no real need to share it with others outside their church circle. Reflecting on this much later, Chen knew he had been thinking with his heart and not his head when it came to Ruolan. But he had been young at the time, and he couldn't see the dangers this might pose for their relationship.

Another thing that should have raised a red flag was Ruolan's strong political connections and a national pride that was almost obsessive. Chen thought her great devotion to China was an admirable trait except for the times it got them into arguments that could have no end. She was for a stronger communist-based government, but Chen wasn't. She argued for less cultural influence from the West, but Chen was for it. Ruolan also felt the country would be better off economically with a longer working day. But Chen remembered his long days in the factory as a young man and insisted that this was not the answer. "Allowing people to operate their own small family businesses is the real ticket to a brighter economy in China's future," he said.

There were those who tried to reason with Chen about Ruolan. She was young and was such a recent convert. What did Chen really know about her or her background? Wouldn't it be better to give their relationship more time before he allowed himself to be so completely taken in by her charms? And her political background? Wasn't that a concern for him?

Chen did not want to admit that those issues could get in the way of his and Ruolan's happiness. For him, life was one grand horizon of blue sky, and Ruolan was at the center of it. He now found himself falling irresistibly, uncontrollably head over heels in love with this beautiful woman.

Theirs was a whirlwind romance, and before very long, they were married. Every day brought sunshine for Chen now, and to him life could not be better. But this was not to last.

In 1949, the new communist government Ruolan had wanted came to power. The arrival of revolutionary Mao Zedong on the political scene brought much enthusiastic praise, especially from the young at heart.

But for Christians everywhere in China, there could have been no greater disaster! Now all churches had to go underground to meet in secret, and that made it very difficult for Chen and Ruolan to worship with their fellow believers. They had to be very careful when and with whom they worshiped. Usually, they met in unexpected places, places the government spies would never think to look, and the locations were changed weekly. But even then, infiltrators were on the prowl befriending Christians, looking for unsuspecting believers so they could entrap them in the act of worship.

Chen's faith thrived during these trying times because his upbringing had been a hard one. Even under duress, he found ways to earn a meager living and still be a witness for Jesus. He secured precious copies of the Bible or Ellen White books and sold them to people who expressed a need for spiritual things. If the people couldn't afford them, he often gave them away. He also worked as a tutor teaching children how to read, then gave Bible studies to their parents late at night after the lessons were done. He didn't make much money in these missionary activities, but he was helping to bring the gospel to those who were searching for truth.

For Ruolan, it was different. Her Christian roots did not run deep. She had been a Christian for only a short time and did not feel a burden to share the gospel with others as Chen did. She could not understand Chen's great desire to witness for Jesus, and when the fires of persecution began to heat up, her faith weakened. Why did Chen have to spend all his time doing missionary work, she would ask him. Why didn't he get a job like everyone else that would pay him regular wages?

And when she gave birth to a son, Zian, their first child, times became even harder; they could no longer subsist on the simple wages Chen brought home. Day by day, Ruolan urged Chen to get a real job that could support them, and he finally agreed.

He found a job working on an assembly line in a pharmaceutical plant, and the pay was quite good, as post-World War II wages went. However, the new communist government had seized all factories, and from the very start Chen could see there would be conflicts. The factory required a six-day workweek, and employees were expected to work on Saturdays. This was something Chen knew he would never be willing to do. How could he dishonor God by violating the holy Sabbath day?

Chen decided to ask for Sabbaths off before that first weekend arrived. He would make his wishes known and find out where he stood with his supervisor, or he would lose his job trying. The supervisor refused but surprised Chen by sending him to another branch of the factory. This decision was a windfall for Chen and gave him hope as to what God might have in store for him.

The manager at Chen's new job found him to be a hard-working man. Chen always showed up early and often stayed late. He was organized and efficient and got along with the other workers. He was also honest, something the new communist government highly valued. This put Chen in good standing with his new supervisor, and when Chen asked for his Sabbaths off, the manager agreed. Even more surprisingly, Chen was allowed to work five days a week instead of six, with his Sabbaths off, but with the same salary.

That first Sabbath, Chen's personal testimony at church was one of praise for the incredible blessings God had granted him at his new workplace. Everyone rejoiced with him and Ruolan. Things seemed to be looking up for the young couple, and this strengthened their faith in God's care for them.

Chen glanced at Ruolan and little Zian sitting beside him in the home church, and thanked God for His goodness. To have a loving wife and son, and a good job where he could earn a fair wage and witness for his faith was more than he had hoped for.

In 1953, the church in Shanghai opened a new seminary to train Bible workers. Young men everywhere came to the school to train as missionaries for God. The classes were held at night to accommodate men who were working day jobs, and Chen was among them. This began a new phase for Chen that would change his life forever.

The night school was a blessing for everyone, and Chen did well. In fact, he proved to be such a good student that he was soon being asked to help write the Bible lessons used each night.

Unfortunately, after nearly a year at his job in the pharmaceutical factory, he ran into trouble. The manager was transferred and a new boss came to the factory. Mr. Jiang was a short, stocky man with hunched shoulders and a face chiseled in stone. "I don't think he's smiled a day in his life," Chen told Ruolan that first day with the new manager.

Mr. Jiang knew nothing about Chen's previous arrangements for having Sabbaths off, nor did he care. Of course, Chen didn't know that, and he assumed he would be allowed Sabbath privileges as before, but he was wrong.

Chapter 4

That first Sabbath under the new manager, Chen worshiped with his regular church group, never giving his job a thought. Sabbath was his favorite day of the week. On this special day, he and his family enjoyed singing the simple hymns, reading from Scripture, and socializing with like-minded believers as they worshiped their Maker. They could share their problems with one another as they celebrated God's holy day. They could testify in praise that God's goodness was the reason for their hope of salvation.

Through it all, Chen was blissfully unaware of an impending snag at work that would soon disrupt his life. On Monday morning, he found a notice on the factory bulletin board with his name in bold letters announcing that he could no longer miss work on Saturdays. Chen was dumbstruck and stood for the longest time staring at the notice. God had been blessing him with Sabbath privileges for over a year, and he had come to take them for granted, but now he could see that the free ride was over. Satan was on the warpath. It was just a matter of time before his job would be on the line too. If he were to remain faithful in his devotion to God's holy Sabbath, he would probably soon be out of work.

However, the following Sabbath Chen went to church again, disregarding the clear warning that had been posted on the bulletin board for almost a week now. He would honor the Sabbath no matter what. He would be true to God's commandment even if the heavens should fall.

But in spite of his convictions, that entire Sabbath during the worship services he found his mind wandering as he thought of his boss's warning. Nagging doubts kept pressing themselves in around the edges of his mind. Would the factory manager lower the boom on him come Monday morning?

But when Monday morning came and he showed up for work as usual, to his surprise the boss said nothing. All that day as he fulfilled his responsibilities on the assembly line, Chen was on pins and needles contemplating the inevitable confrontation with the boss. And when quitting time came and he punched out at the time clock, the manager had still not approached him.

As the days passed that week and nothing was said, Chen began to think the manager would give him a pass and allow him to continue skipping work on the Sabbath.

However, on Friday Chen's supervisor pulled him aside and warned him sternly that if he didn't come to work the next day, he would be asked to resign. Chen's heart fell, knowing his worst fears had finally been realized. What could he do? His choices were limited. Be true to his convictions and look elsewhere for work, or work Saturdays and keep his job? There was no question in his mind what he had to do, but that didn't make the outcome any less difficult. He knew he had to honor the Sabbath, yet he knew he needed the job to support his wife and son.

Chen decided to keep the Sabbath, of course, and told the manager of his decision. "I have no other choice," Chen told him. "I owe that to my Creator. He has made the Sabbath day holy and asked that I rest on that day in worship. No matter the cost, I cannot dishonor Him by working on Sabbath."

The manager stared at Chen. "Then I guess you know what you have to do come Monday. Bring me your letter of resignation," he added flatly. "It's either your Saturdays off or the job. You can't have it both ways."

He shrugged and turned away coldly, and Chen knew that unless God somehow intervened, this would be his last day of work at the factory.

The next morning dawned clear and bright, and Chen thought he had never seen a better day to be alive. The birds sang more cheerfully as he walked the short distance to worship with the group of believers. The spring cherry blossoms in the city park were even more fragrant than he remembered they could be. However, once again Chen found it hard to relax and really enjoy this day of rest he loved best. Everything seemed to be a blur as he went back again and again to the conversation he'd had with the factory manager. *It's either your Saturdays off or the job. You can't have it both ways.*

And worshiping God at church was a battle today. The singing he loved, though he wasn't much of a singer, but today he found it hard to make the songs of praise genuine. Reading scriptures for the group seemed to be a charade since his mind was preoccupied with the looming likelihood of losing his job. He gave no testimony because he was afraid his lack of faith in God might show.

And Chen had to wonder, *Does Ruolan know of the struggle that is tearing me apart inside?* She had not come to church today because she wasn't feeling well, she'd said. He guessed she knew that something wasn't right because of the way she kept looking at him over breakfast. There had been tension in the air between them, and several times when she had asked him questions, she'd had

Chains in China

to repeat herself. Chen didn't want to admit it, but things had been decidedly cool between them of late.

But if she suspected something, she hadn't expressed it or managed to put her finger on it, and for this Chen was glad. He didn't want to have to wrestle with his coming calamity and break the bad news to her as well. There would be time enough for that on Monday.

On Monday, Chen's supervisor, Mr. Jiang, was in his office waiting for Chen. He said nothing as he sat at his desk staring over the top of his wire rims, but the look in his eyes spoke volumes. He had a confidence in his eyes that could not be denied, as if he clearly expected that Chen had changed his mind.

Chen stood there shifting his weight from one foot to the other, wondering how best to break the news, as if putting off the announcement would somehow make the outcome easier. But there was no good or easy way to say what needed to be said. "I've decided to write the letter of resignation," Chen finally announced. He stared at Mr. Jiang. This was the biggest decision he had ever made. "I cannot give up my Sabbaths and my day to worship God. I was hoping you would somehow change your mind and let me have the days off, sir, but I guess that's not going to happen, is it?"

"I could say the same thing to you," the manager said incredulously. "Actually, I'm quite surprised. After thinking it over this weekend, I had thought your answer this morning would be different." He paused to take a sip of tea from a cup sitting on his desk. "You're a family man, aren't you? Your wife, Ruolan? What does she have to say about all this?"

Chen glanced warily at Mr. Jiang. What did the manager mean? How did he know Ruolan's name? Was Chen missing something? Was this some kind of setup?

"I hear you may be getting a divorce soon," Mr. Jiang kept on. "That can't be good news for anyone! Think what that will mean for you and your son."

"A divorce!" Chen stammered. "What are you talking about?" His mind reeled and his vision blurred as he stared at Mr. Jiang behind his desk. Where was the factory manager going with this latest quip? "My wife doesn't know anything about this!" Chen finally said.

"She does now," Mr. Jiang replied. "We've been in conversation with her for quite some time, and she has something she'd like to say to you." The manager picked up the phone on his desk and dialed a number. "Comrade Ruolan, this is Mr. Jiang at the pharmaceutical factory. Your husband is here. You may speak to him now." Mr. Jiang handed the phone to Chen. "Go ahead. Tell her of your decision," he ordered coldly.

Chen stared at the manager unbelievingly. His mouth dropped open as he took the phone. At first, he couldn't speak, but Ruolan's voice was calling to him incessantly over the phone. He could hear her voice faint and far away, but to him it all seemed like some bad dream. "Chen! Chen!" she was almost shouting. "Are you listening to me?"

"I'm here," Chen finally stammered. "I can hear you! You don't have to shout." He had finally gotten his bearings, and it annoyed him that she should treat him so. Where was the dutiful, respectful woman she had promised to be when they fell in love and married a few short years ago?

"Tell me it isn't true!" Chen could hear the ice in Ruolan's voice over the phone. "Tell me it hasn't come to this! You would rather let Zian and me go hungry than work Saturdays?"

"Let you go hungry?" Chen couldn't believe his ears. "You're not going to go hungry even if I don't keep this job. You know I'll never let that happen! What kind of a husband do think I am?"

"A perfectly crazy one!" she snorted, and he could hear her voice turning on him now. "I'll not have a husband who chooses his religion over his wife and son!"

Chapter 5

"What is going on, Ruolan?" Chen lowered his voice as he glanced at Mr. Jiang. "You know my convictions about the Sabbath. You've always known them. Why this sudden concern over something you know I won't bend on?"

"Because times are hard, and I don't think it will matter to God that you work once in a while on the Sabbath! Not when He knows your family needs the money!"

"But it won't be once in a while, Ruolan," Chen was getting irritated, and it bothered him that she was insisting he have this conversation over the phone in public. "They want me to work every Sabbath, and you know I can't do that."

"Can't do it, or won't do it?" she argued.

"Can't do it? Won't do it? What's the difference?" He was getting angry again at her persistence. "I'm not going to have this conversation over the phone."

"Are you going to give your manager a letter of resignation?" she demanded coolly. "Mr. Jiang said that's what you intend to do."

"When I get home, I'll explain everything."

"Oh no you won't!" she replied. By now, her voice had taken on the proportions of an iceberg-like chill. "If you submit that letter, don't bother coming home."

Chen couldn't believe his ears! What was happening? What had come over Ruolan? How could she be treating him so harshly, and over something as precious as the Sabbath? "What do you mean, don't come home?" He finally found his voice. "It's my home!"

"Not anymore it isn't! Not if you choose the Sabbath over your family," she said emphatically. "I've already drawn up the divorce papers. If you sign that resignation letter, you can sign away your marriage while you're at it!"

She hung up on him, and Chen just stood there holding the receiver in his hand. Mr. Jiang was staring at him, waiting for his final verdict, but when Chen didn't say anything, the manager became all business again.

"Well, I guess we're just wasting our time here. Let's get this over with," he added, pulling out a sheet of paper and a pen. He pushed them across the desk toward Chen.

"I don't understand," Chen finally stammered. His shoulders slumped as he took the pen, holding it motionless. "What's come over my wife? She was never like this."

"I'll tell you what's come over her," Mr. Jiang said as he took out a file folder from his desk and began going through its contents. "She has finally come to her senses and come back to what she loves best. I don't know what kind of a Christian she was, but she is a very good communist."

"Communist?" Chen stared at Mr. Jiang's leering grin. His mind went back to some of the arguments they'd had over how the government should be run, and he marveled at how naïve he had been for not seeing it. How could he have been so blind to her political loyalties? How could he have disregarded all the plain counsel others had given him to beware of her background? No doubt, the communist party had convinced Ruolan to work with the factory and Mr. Jiang to put pressure on Chen. Evidently, she had agreed, and Mr. Jiang had known about this all along. But what had they done to Ruolan to get her to make a 180 turn in her previous convictions as a Christian? She was not a weak person, though it was true she had been a Christian for only a short time.

"I'm going to write the letter regardless of the consequences," Chen said, finally picking up the pen, "but I just have one question. What did they do to Ruolan to get her to turn against me?"

"They were not kind," Mr. Jiang could not look Chen in the eye, "but I can tell you this much, I think it had something to do with your son."

"Those dirty scoundrels!" Chen muttered under his breath as he realized just what that meant. The communist leaders must have threatened Ruolan about the safety of their son, and that made Chen angry. Would they come and take little Zian away to remove him from the influences of Christianity? Chen knew the communist leaders did this kind of thing often to frighten people into obedience.

But right now, he knew there was nothing he could do. A line had been drawn in the sand by the communists in a calculated move, daring him to step over it. He had done just that in his efforts to honor God and the Sabbath, and now he was going to pay a heavy price. Would it have changed his mind to know all that would arise from his decision? Maybe not, but Chen would never know for sure because by the time the dust had settled over the whole issue, it was too late to turn back. By the day's end, he had lost his job, his wife, his son, and his home.

Chains in China

That night as he lay on the floor in the home of a kind friend who had taken him in, Chen stared up at the ceiling, once again asking himself where he had gone wrong. What could he have done differently? But he always came back to the same conclusion. He had married Ruolan knowing their differences, and maybe that had been his biggest blunder. But the Sabbath? He would never give up his convictions about the sacredness of the day, and he would never give up the right and privilege to worship God as the fourth commandment required.

"Remember the Sabbath day by keeping it holy," Chen began reciting the well-known verses in his mind. *"Six days you shall labor and do all your work, but the seventh day is a Sabbath to the Lord your God. On it you shall not do any work, neither you, nor your son or daughter, nor your male or female servant, nor your animals, nor any foreigner residing in your towns. For in six days the Lord made the heavens and the earth, the sea, and all that is in them, but he rested on the seventh day. Therefore the Lord blessed the Sabbath day and made it holy"* (Exodus 20:8–11, NIV).

The words brought him comfort somehow. He didn't know how that could be. His devotion to the fourth commandment was the reason he no longer had a family or a home. The job he had lost was not important in his mind, really. He could always get another one sometime, somewhere. But his wife and son? They were his home, and they brought him happiness. The hopelessness of such a thought almost overwhelmed him, but then he stopped himself as he really thought about that notion. Was there something wrong with that picture? Was it true that only a wife, son, and home could bring him happiness?

Chen watched the dancing shapes of shadows playing tag with one another on the ceiling. Who would guess that the light of a dim street lamp and the branches of a tree outside the veranda could make such strange caricatures on the ceiling above him? Maybe his life was like that. Maybe God was working in mysterious ways using a variety of circumstances to bring about a wider, deeper plan for Chen's life. After all, if he put others above God, what was the point of claiming he was a Christian? Hadn't Jesus warned His followers about that very thing? Hadn't Jesus Himself given His all when He left the Father and came to die for the human race?

More Scripture came to mind as Chen continued staring at the ceiling. *"You will be betrayed even by parents and brothers, relatives and friends. . . . And you will be hated by all for My name's sake"* (Luke 21:16, 17, NKJV). *" 'A man's enemies will be those of his own household.' He who loves father or mother more than Me is not worthy of Me. And he who loves son or daughter more than Me is not worthy of Me. And he who does not take his cross and follow after Me is not worthy of Me"* (Matthew 10:36–38, NKJV).

Chen didn't want to be betrayed by family members, but he didn't want to live without God in his life either. That would be worse than death itself. He closed his eyes and tried to shut out such thoughts. He hated the thought of having to go on without Ruolan and the company of little Zian. Maybe Ruolan would change her mind. Maybe she would come looking for him in the morning. Or maybe it would take her a few days to mull things over. Maybe in a week or so she would come to her senses and realize that the family blood in her veins ran thicker than her loyalties to some government ideology.

Maybe, but maybe not. If there was one thing Chen did know about Ruolan, it was her stubborn pride. She would stick this thing out longer than most women would, and by that time, the communist officials would have gotten a real hold on her. Who knew what measures they were taking at this very moment to secure their wishes? Who knew what lies they were telling her about him?

Chen was just a young man of twenty-six, but already his life was a failure, it seemed. He had lost his job and home. His wife of just a few years had left him and taken their only son with her. Would he ever see his little son, Zian, again? He had thought he was a good husband and father, but what had any of those fine qualities gotten him? Without a doubt, he had hit the bottom rung of life's ladder.

Chen pondered the cause of all his problems. Evidently, Ruolan's old ties with the communist party had proven to be too much for her. Clearly, her love for the church had been only superficial, and now he was reaping the whirlwind for his decisions. Now he must once again be a bachelor without a family.

Was his devotion to service and the church worth all the pain and heartache he was suffering? His father had suffered from the sacrifices he had made to see that others heard the good news of the gospel, and what had it gotten him? Nothing but a life on the road with no real place to call home.

Chapter 6

Chen rubbed his tired eyes and straightened up from the typewriter where he sat in a small room of the Shanghai Chinese Church. He leaned back in his straight-backed wooden chair and took a deep breath to clear his lungs. The smell of alcohol from the mimeograph machine was strong, making him a bit lightheaded.

For six weeks now, he had been translating a copy of *The Great Controversy,* a book about the history of the Christian church. But his typewriter was so old, and his fingers had grown sore from all the pecking at its rusty keys. He had already completed three hundred pages of English into Chinese and still had about four hundred to go.

A lone moth fluttered near the kerosene lamp on his worktable, drawn irresistibly to the dancing firelight. *What a concept,* thought Chen. The light of this kerosene lamp was like the light of the gospel to the people of China. Like this little moth, if people were truly searching for truth, they would see the light of God in the precious books he was translating.

He glanced at the half-typed sheet now in the typewriter. His efforts seemed so feeble. Pecking out characters one at a time on the old typewriter made words on his paper. These words made sentences and paragraphs. The paragraphs turned into pages and chapters. When each book was finally finished after months of tiresome work, it was a triumph indeed. But the process was so time-consuming.

He couldn't deny that these books he labored on day and night were sacred. The inspiration and hard work invested in the special books had cost the church much. Chen's own labor seemed insignificant in comparison to the men and women who had sacrificed so much to get them out to the public. Bible workers had risked their freedom, walking the streets of Shanghai and other Chinese cities to sell the books. Some of these soldiers for Christ had been imprisoned in their efforts to keep the books safe. Some had even paid with their lives.

Chen glanced at the clock on the wall. The hour was late, already 10:00 P.M., and he knew he should stop for the night, but how could he? His pastor, Lin

David, sat at a desk nearby still going strong on a typewriter of his own. His current project was a copy of *The Desire of Ages,* a book about the life of Jesus.

Pastor Lin was a monument of spiritual strength, a giant in the Chinese Christian community. For fourteen years, he had been leading this band of Seventh-day Adventists in Shanghai, China, and now the church in Eastern China was growing in spite of persecution. The work had been so successful in fact, that the "church" had appointed nine men to work with Pastor Lin in his plans for evangelism. Everyone called them the "board" because they made all the final decisions about the business of the church, but there was little status in such titles. Their main mission was to get Bibles and Spirit of Prophecy books into the hands of honest, hard-working people who were searching for truth, and the only way to do that was to get out on the street.

Many of the board members were young, not much older than Chen himself. Pastor Lin had told Chen that he would probably soon be a part of that board because of all his hard work to help get the books printed. But Chen didn't feel worthy of such a calling. How could he be part of the board when his own life was a disaster, a failure in every way? He had nothing to offer the church in the way of leadership. He was not wise, or rich, or influential in the community. No one on the street would call him a success, that much was sure. Because of his determination to keep the Sabbath, he had lost his job, his wife, and his child all in one day. The experience had shaken him to the core, and he wondered if he would ever again be the strong, confident man he had once been.

It all seemed so discouraging, but Pastor Lin reminded Chen that Jesus had spoken of such things. Christians could expect that the followers of Jesus would be abandoned by their families, become destitute in the things of this world, and even become homeless for their efforts to stand for the truths of the gospel.

Evangelism for any Christian church was forbidden under the new Chinese regime, so the Seventh-day Adventist Church had gone underground, as the government police were calling it. From week to week now, no one really knew where believers could or should meet. The Seventh-day Adventist Church building was out of the question even in the dead of night. Government spies were everywhere. They lurked in every crowd, and they often infiltrated Christian meetings held in secret.

But that didn't stop the believers from meeting. News of secret services spread via word of mouth. When informants gave Pastor Lin tips that the government soldiers or secret police were close to discovering their hideouts, they would simply move their meetings to another location. Even the board of church leaders no longer dared meet in the church.

Chen yawned and glanced toward his cot in the corner of the room where he was typing. Just a month ago, Pastor Lin had made him an offer he couldn't refuse. In exchange for a place to sleep, Chen was to serve as a security guard to help prevent burglaries at the church. No one worshiped at the church anymore, but that didn't matter. It made a perfectly good home for Chen, and the angels of God were with him in this place. He couldn't have asked for a better home.

He was grateful to Pastor Lin for taking him on again like this. Of course, he knew better than to think that Pastor Lin actually needed him at the church for security reasons. He felt ashamed for having left his position as a Bible worker to take the job at the pharmaceutical factory. But he had been short on money, and Ruolan had been insistent. It had not been a good situation for a young man with a family, and Ruolan's faith had been weak, making it all the harder to stay on with Pastor Lin at the church.

But now he was back. After Chen had accepted the pastor's offer to be a security guard at the church, Pastor Lin had asked if Chen might help translate Bibles and books using one of the old typewriters at the church. "I liked your idea when you mentioned it several years ago," Pastor Lin admitted, "but we just didn't have the equipment or the people to do it right. But now, thanks to you, we have a good operation going here at the church that can translate and publish more than half a dozen books a year."

What an opportunity! What an idea! That had been three hundred pages ago and many nights of sleeping on the cot. It had turned out to be a fine proposition for everyone involved. Chen was fairly good on a typewriter, and his translating skills were excellent! The going was slow when it came to copy work on a typewriter, but according to Pastor Lin, Chen was "one of the fastest typists ever to help in transcribing the books."

The room where they were now working was an inner room with no windows, so the two of them could work on their books long into the night. The church was no longer in use for public meetings, so the police did not suspect a printing operation was housed there.

Chapter 7

You'd better get some sleep," Pastor Lin echoed Chen's weary thoughts. "We're not going to finish these books tonight. I'd better head home myself," he laughed with a tired smile and blew out the flickering flame of the kerosene lamp on his desk. "If I stay here much longer, my wife will wonder where I am."

"No, she won't," Chen laughed too. "You do this most every night." He followed Pastor Lin out to lock and bar the church doors.

"I have to go see the widow Lanfen tomorrow," Pastor Lin said, turning one last time in the darkness. "She is failing fast. Her daughter begged me to go see her last week and then again this past Sabbath, so I simply cannot put it off another day. I hope to visit her and one other family in the morning, and then later maybe I'll get out to sell some books. I'm glad we decided to ask you to help type books here at the church instead of sending you out on the streets like the rest of us. Someone has to keep the books rolling off the presses."

He laid a hand on Chen's shoulder and bowed his head instinctively. "Lord, protect my brother here tonight at the church," he prayed. "May Your angels guard him and our beloved church." Then he was gone.

Chen retired to his army cot and knelt by its side before blowing out his lamp for the night. He loved working for the church in this way and felt honored to serve God in times of persecution, but being all alone was hard too. He tried not to think of his wife and small son, but it was almost impossible. He loved his wife. She had been such a good woman, serving with him in one of the Shanghai churches, and his son was the apple of his eye. He grew sad as he thought of all that had gone wrong.

"I must trust You, Lord," he sighed as a stray tear stole its way down his face in the darkness. "I must believe that You can bring good out of these great trials that have come into my life." And then he slept the sleep of exhaustion for one who had worked so many hours.

The next morning, he awoke before dawn to the sound of a gentle tapping at the door. It was Manchu, one of the Bible workers who had come to get a fresh supply of Bibles and books to sell. Chen was glad to see Manchu and offered him something to eat, but Manchu declined, afraid the police might see him coming and going even at this early hour if he stayed.

Chen helped him fill his shoulder pack with books from their secret hiding place under the floorboards of the church. Then, after a hurried prayer in the darkness, Manchu rushed out into the morning mists with his backpack of books on his shoulder.

Other than Pastor Lin, Manchu was the first person to have shown up at the church in almost a week. Even the other "board" members never showed up at the church anymore except to get books when they ran out, and then only under cover of darkness.

All that morning, Chen worked on his rickety typewriter, finishing page after page by the light of his kerosene lamp in the windowless room. In his work of translating, when he came to difficult spots in the text, he had to jot his thoughts down on paper before transferring the characters to the typewriter. If he made a mistake in his typing, he had to take a razor blade and scrape the carbon ink off the paper, then correct the mistake. By noon, he had finished four more pages, stopping only long enough to eat a light lunch of steamed rice with chopped cabbage and carrots.

Then it was back to work again. Those long hours at the old typewriter by light of the dim lamp were tiresome and intense. Sometimes the only thing that kept him going was his devotion to evangelism and the thought that Pastor Lin was counting on him. And, of course, he knew he was helping print books to save souls for the kingdom of God. That was the most important reason of all.

No one else stopped by the church all day, not even Pastor Lin, so Chen was quite alone. By late afternoon, he was feeling in need of fresh air and decided to risk a walk. He left through the back door of the church, glancing both ways to be sure no one was watching him, and then scooted down a back alley.

It was wonderful to be out in the cool autumn air again. He realized that he had not been out like this for several days now, and it felt so good. He wandered down to the market where the vendors were selling their wares and foodstuffs. At one shop, he saw all kinds of paper lanterns, and at another, brooms for sweeping. A little farther down were clothing shops, and then there was the outdoor food market. Baskets of rice sat in rows under awnings, and piles of cabbages, carrots, and onions reminded him he hadn't eaten a full home-cooked meal in days. Farther down was the meat market with its ducks and geese and pigs hanging from hooks overhead.

By now, the shadows of evening were coming, and Chen turned his steps homeward. Soon it would be dark. When Pastor Lin returned, Chen wanted to be at the church to greet him and have some hot wonton stew waiting for him.

Chains in China

Chen walked back to the church by a different route, taking longer than necessary. This was one of his many strategies to avoid being followed in case the police suspected him of being a church worker. He always carried his official identification papers with him and tried to look inconspicuous, so he wasn't too worried about being stopped. He was only afraid they might follow him to the church and discover the scores of valuable religious books stashed there.

The sun had set over the red clay rooftops of Shanghai as Chen had approached the little alley that ran past the back door of the church. He had returned undetected, and he thanked God for that. Within minutes, he was back inside lighting a small fire in the charcoal oven to boil water for the wonton stew he planned to make.

But suddenly he heard shouting and running feet. He had been working under cover of darkness with no lights on except the fire under the pot, so he felt safe enough. Quickly, he went to the one small window high in a wall facing the alley, and what he saw there made his heart stop. Pastor Lin was in the alley surrounded by four government police with red armbands on their coat sleeves. One of the police had the pastor by the arm and was shaking him.

Chen froze! What should he do? Had the police followed Pastor Lin here? Had they come to raid the church? In an instant, he thought of the Bibles and books hidden under the floorboards. There was no time to guess what he needed to do—he knew he must act fast! Seconds mattered now. Could he escape from the church and smuggle some of the Bibles out without being detected? Not likely. The police no doubt had the church building surrounded by now! Unless, of course, they didn't know he was in the church.

Quickly, Chen made his decision! He would escape—if he could—and take as many books with him as possible. It seemed the only way. He snatched up his shoulder pack and ran to the corner where the wooden floorboards were loose. Pulling the boards away, he jumped down into the crawl space beneath the floor and began loading Bibles and books into the pack. The pack was large, but he was surprised at how many books were going into it—more than he would have thought possible.

In less than a minute, it seemed, Chen was up and out of the crawl space again, returning the boards to their place. His eyes darted around the room. He must leave no telltale signs of the hiding place behind. Quickly, he dragged a rug across the floor to cover the loose boards, and then set a small table and chair on the rug. He then thought of the manuscripts for the books he and Pastor Lin had been typing on the typewriters. If the police saw the freshly typed pages, they would be suspicious and start looking for the precious books and Bibles. They might even tear up the floorboards in search of the books if they suspected they could be hidden there.

Chapter 8

The police were still shouting in the alley, and it occurred to Chen that Pastor Lin might be trying to stall them so he could get out in time to save himself. And the books? Had Pastor Lin guessed that Chen might try to rescue some of the books? Probably. Chen and Pastor Lin thought much alike.

Chen grabbed the unfinished pages in the typewriters and the stack of manuscripts on a table. Stuffing them into the shoulder pack with the books, he snatched up his coat and ran to the front door of the church. How to get out of the church now was the biggest problem. When he looked out the front window, he was surprised to see no one there. No police. No one even standing around to see what the commotion was all about at the back of the church.

He put on his coat, pulled the hood up over his head, and darted out into the darkness. The cold night air filled his lungs, adding to the excitement of the moment. He glanced this way and that. Where could he go? Where should he hide? He didn't know exactly what he should do, but he knew what he could not do. He could not go back to the church, even to collect the few personal belongings he had left behind. It was too dangerous! Spies and informants would be watching him, no doubt, and would guess that he might come back when the excitement of the raid was over. Should he go to the homes of the other Bible workers or board members? Was it safe at their homes, or had they been rounded up too? Chen knew he hadn't a moment to waste as he hurried up the street toward the busiest part of town. In that part of the city, he could easily lose himself in the crowd.

As he turned the corner, he glanced back one more time to catch a glimpse of the church, the place he had come to love. Would he ever return? He knew there was nothing for him in Shanghai anymore. No job, no home, no family. And now no church. With such harsh restrictions imposed by the new government, he must leave the city. He must start over again. He must go somewhere far away where no one knew him. But where? Telling himself he needed to go was one thing. Actually doing it was another. There were so many unknowns.

In the east, the moon was now rising pale-orange over the city. *God will not forsake me,* Chen thought as he shifted the shoulder pack to his other shoulder. He stopped to lean against a lamppost and closed his eyes as he thought of the words Pastor Lin had recited many times from Scripture. *"You will be brought before governors and kings as witnesses,"* he said. *"You will be hated by everyone because of me, but the one who stands firm to the end will be saved"* (Matthew 10:18, 22, NIV).

The thought of such things now was depressing, and yet, in a strange sort of way, the verses were encouraging. Jesus had told them these things would happen, but He had also promised that good would eventually come from it all. Hadn't He said, "Be faithful until death and I will give you a crown of life" (Revelation 2:10)?

When Chen thought of it that way, he felt a strange peace come over him. He was no longer fearful of the unknown, and everything somehow seemed more hopeful. He was worried about Pastor Lin back there with the police but prayed the police would do him no harm. Surely God would be with him as he and the church went through the flames of persecution. That had been the way things were before Chen began working at the church, and by God's grace, it would always be so. Pastor Lin and the others were strong and faithful. They were godly men and women ready to stand for God no matter the cost.

Chen wandered the streets for several hours, not sure where he should go. He needed a place to stay for a few days until he could decide what to do next. Finally, he thought of an elderly sister, a Mrs. Ah Lam, who had always been kind to him in the local church. Did he dare stop at her home? Would she take him in? Would she be willing to take a chance and let him hide out at her home for a while?

Thankfully, Mrs. Ah Lam accepted him in when he knocked on the door of her home late that night. She welcomed him warmly and fed him some savory wonton soup. Then she gave him a mat and a place to sleep on the floor. Chen was touched by her kindness. It made him feel good to know there were people in the church who loved him and cared about his safety.

But even here in the home of Mrs. Ah Lam, he knew it wasn't safe. The police would know there were other church members in the community. They had their sources, and they might come looking for him.

By noon the next day, Chen learned that all ten of the board members had been arrested on charges of espionage and illegal trafficking of religion. Chen knew those charges were ludicrous, but he also knew now that his fears had been well founded. It was not safe for him any longer in Shanghai. He must flee the city. A train would probably be best, though he didn't have much money for travel.

Chen pulled his money pouch from his pocket and counted the few Chinese yuan in it. Should he go live with his parents? That was quite a distance, if he had enough money to make it. He counted the bills again. It was clear there would be no money for food.

He thanked Mrs. Ah Lam for her kind hospitality and left her home early that afternoon. The police might come looking for him any time, and he didn't dare put Mrs. Ah Lam's life in danger as well. In his shoulder pack, he took the only belongings he owned in this world: a few clothes, a dozen cabbage rolls Mrs. Ah Lam gave him, and, of course, his Bible.

As he stood on the street pondering his next move, an intercity bus pulled up to the corner and stopped. *Now there is an idea,* Chen thought to himself as he watched passengers get on and off. *Why not take the bus?* It would be cheaper, and he could ride it as far as it would take him. That way he would be sure to get far away from the communist police who might be looking for him.

Without another thought, Chen hopped on to the bus and settled into a window seat. "I hope this is a good idea, Lord," he whispered. "Take me where You need me. I want to serve You someplace, but I think that someplace is not here right now."

The bus pulled away shortly, and with it went Chen on a new adventure for God. But where should he go? He still had no real plan, no answer about where he might make a new start for himself. More importantly, what should he do with his life from this day forward? Should he train to be a pastor? Chen seemed to be well fitted for such a calling. He loved to study his Bible. He loved translating and publishing books, and more than anything, he wanted to share the gospel with others. But how could he do this—and where?

Chapter 9

Chen awoke suddenly as though from a long dream. He rubbed the foggy sleep from his eyes and turned to stare out through the dusty window. Where was he? What was he doing on this bus?

And then he remembered. He had boarded the bus to get away from the communist police. His life was in disarray. He had left his job to honor the Sabbath, and his wife had then left him, taking little Zian with her. He had begun working at the church in Shanghai translating books by Ellen White and was making real progress until the police captured Pastor Lin. They then rounded up the rest of the church evangelism crew, punishing them for illegal trafficking of the Seventh-day Adventist faith through the sale of religious books. Chen himself had narrowly escaped capture by the government police and was now on the run. He knew thinking such self-defeating thoughts was dangerous, but he was discouraged.

The bus stopped and started at many small towns on the road, giving Chen time to ponder God's leading in his life. Was it possible that through all these trials God was leading him to a greater calling? What did God have in store for him next? Where would he end up, and what role would he play in spreading the gospel he loved so much? One thing was sure: he must bring others to Jesus at any cost. He must be the faithful soldier God was asking him to be. He must move on.

The bus he was riding now slowed to a stop beside the road in a little town called Wu Xi. Chen got off to stretch his legs. He glanced around at the neat streets with red-tiled roofs and quaint little shops. Children ran and played in the narrow lanes and alleys. Old women squatted in the open town square selling their wares. Farmers with pointed hats walked the streets carrying their hoes and rakes. And interestingly enough, Chen saw no police.

What a pleasant little town, Chen thought. And then it struck him! Wu Xi seemed like a nice enough place to live. Why not stay? Maybe this was a place where he could live and witness for God. Maybe Wu Xi was the haven he had been looking for to serve God in peace. Maybe here he could grow into the worker and leader God wanted him to be. *This town is a perfect place to hide,* Chen thought. It was off the main roads with a small population of maybe less than one or two thousand, he guessed.

Minutes later when the bus drove away, Chen was not on it, and a new chapter opened in his life. As he stood on a street corner surveying the small town, he wondered if there were any Adventists in it and if he could find them. The town was small enough that anyone would know if such a people lived here. And yet it struck him that there might be others like himself who were hiding from government officials. He would like to find the Adventists, but he didn't want to draw unnecessary attention their way.

It was Friday now, so the next day was the Sabbath. Surely, if he walked these streets on the Sabbath and the Adventists were worshiping together somewhere, he would find them. They would no doubt be meeting privately in a home.

Chen was very hungry after the long bus ride but had almost no money left after paying the bus fare. Grudgingly, he ate two of the egg rolls in his backpack. That was all he could spare, he felt, or he wouldn't have enough to get him through the Sabbath.

That night he slept out under the stars beside a rice stack. The evening was a bit chilly, but he wrapped his coat around him and thanked God it was a dry night.

The next morning, he awoke a bit stiff but glad to greet the Sabbath day. He bowed his head to thank God for the little bit of food he had and then ate two more egg rolls, noting that there were only two left now. He smiled self-consciously as he brushed the straw from his clothes and ran his fingers through his hair. Without a mirror, he had no idea how he really looked, but one thing was sure—he had slept in the open air beside a rice stack, and that meant he needed to make himself look presentable. His circumstances were far from ideal, but first impressions could be so important. It would never do to show up for worship looking bedraggled and frumpy.

He began walking the short city streets, but of course, the hour was early; he didn't really expect anyone to be gathering for services yet. He realized he was expecting much to be looking for an Adventist group in a town of this size anyway. Surely, there would be other Christians in Wu Xi in small groups maybe, but Seventh-day Adventist worshipers?

He walked the full length of the main street in town and turned down a side street when to his surprise he heard music coming from a house nearby. And it was a familiar hymn they were singing. "Lift up the trumpet and loud let it ring" was wafting clearly down the village streets in the crisp morning air.

Chains in China

Chen ventured near enough to see the singers through an open window and then began singing along with them. "Nations are angry, by this we do know! Jesus is coming again! Knowledge increases, men run to and fro! Jesus is coming again!"

Suddenly, a young girl noticed Chen and pointed at him. He smiled and moved toward the door of the home. If they wished him to join them, they would come to the door and invite him in. If not, well, he would have to move on for now.

But they did ask him in, though they welcomed him cautiously. After all, one could never be too careful during these times. One never knew when a government worker or spy might be lurking in the neighborhood.

Chen felt at home immediately, and before long the small church group of six families was treating him as more than just a visitor. His knowledge of the Bible and experience as a lay pastor made him an authority in their eyes, and a ready-made leader of the group. After a noonday meal, he spent the afternoon with them conducting a Bible study and discovered that two people in the group were ready for baptism. By the end of the day, they had asked him to stay on as the lay pastor of their little Adventist flock.

To make matters even better for Chen, an elderly couple invited him to stay in their home. They had a niece and nephew staying with them too—Chow and Enlai, her brother—so this made for a full house in the small hut they called home. But where there is love, there is joy. Jinhai and his wife, Liu, quickly grew attached to Chen and were soon treating him like a son.

It was a wonderful feeling for him to find a place of refuge so soon after going on the road. Chen had suffered so much in such a short time, and already he had found a family and a home. Without a doubt, God had plans for him in Wu Xi. Now he had a place to stay and a church to serve.

The small group of Adventist believers then went a step further. They offered to pay Chen a small stipend so he could be their pastor and go into evangelism full time. This was a wonderful breakthrough for Chen, an opportunity he had not yet had in his years of service for the church.

He didn't feel fully prepared or qualified to do pastoral work, yet it seemed God was leading, so he accepted. The pay was small, but it was enough for a bachelor, since he was staying in the home of Jinhai and Liu. His expenses were minimal and his needs few.

Not surprisingly, Chen spent most of the Chinese yuan he earned on others. When a child in his congregation needed a new pair of shoes, Chen hired a cobbler in the neighborhood to make them. When an old man in the village needed medical attention, Chen would get him the medicine called for by the village doctor. Young and old were soon coming to him for help. It didn't seem to matter whether they were rich or poor, educated or peasant, Christian or Buddhist. Everyone came to see Chen as a godly man who cared.

Churches had been officially shut down for some time now, so on Sabbaths, Chen worshiped with the Adventist believers in a different home each week. It seemed the right thing to do to avoid confrontation with the authorities. Although Wu Xi was not on the watch list of the communist officials back in Shanghai, it was good to avoid meeting in the same place each week, which would give the officials something to make trouble about.

But Chen made it his habit to find other ways to evangelize. One way was to visit in the homes of those who were sick or in need. This he did regularly, and his visits did wonders for the spirits of the folks in Wu Xi. The love he showed by his acts of kindness was an inspiration to them, and his gentle touch was Christlike.

On these visits, he would read the Bible to them and pray for any special requests they might have. Sometimes he recommended changes in their diet or special herbs they might eat to help them improve their health. Because of his focus on prayer and a healthy diet, he soon became known in the village for his miraculous powers through gifts of healing. Even the non-Adventist Christians and Buddhists could see that he was in touch with heaven.

Chapter 10

One hot summer afternoon, Wencheng, a man in the small church group, called Chen to the bedside of his mother-in-law. She had been bedridden for six months with an illness no doctor could cure. "We have read Bible stories in church of people who were controlled by Satan," he said, "and we think our mother might be possessed by such a demon. If you can do anything, please help us!"

The little Chinese lady was a frail woman, though the firm features of her stern face told him she had once been a woman of prominence. As he knelt by the bedside of the woman and laid his hand on her forehead, she began to shake violently. He could feel her body burning up with fever, but he sensed it wasn't the hot summer temperatures that were causing her illness. This was no ordinary sickness. It was clear Satan was tormenting her. She was not a Christian, so there could be any number of reasons why the devil had power in her life. That she did not know Jesus or the story of salvation was clear, but Chen guessed there was another story here of how she might be serving Satan.

When questioned, the family told him she had, in fact, been using the powers of the dark underworld for years as a clairvoyant medium in the village. She had been working under the spell of supernatural forces as a fortune-teller, just as her mother and grandmother had done before her for generations, and people had been willing to pay for her services. Her name was Yun. She was the authority figure in Wu Xi, and village life had revolved around her. For decades, everyone in the village came to her for advice—when to plant crops; when to harvest; when and whom to marry. No one seemed able to make decisions without first consulting her.

But now in her old age, things were getting worse. The little woman often had seizures and fits of uncontrollable shaking. During these bouts, she sometimes heard voices and would have conversations with someone or something that was in the room but could not be seen.

Everything about the woman seemed to fit the stories of demon possession

Chen had read about in the Bible. Without a doubt, the evil one had put a curse on Yun and was making her life miserable. She had sold her soul to achieve her status, and it was now costing her more than she had bargained for. As long as she was serving Satan, she would never be well. As long as Satan was in control of her body and mind, she was a lost soul.

Chen knew that there was much at stake here in the village of Wu Xi. If the message of salvation was going to reach into the lives of these pagans who did not know Jesus, then it was going to have to begin here and now with this woman. The God of heaven was going to have to reveal Himself mightily and win in this encounter with the prince of darkness.

The little woman turned to stare at Chen. "What do you want with us here?" Her voice was heavy and her eyes glassy, as though she were looking right through him. Chen felt the temperature in the room grow cool, and it sent frightening shivers down his spine. Though he couldn't see the enemy, he knew that Satan was indeed here in this room ready to challenge anyone's right to help this woman.

Help me, Lord, Chen prayed, his skin prickling at the dramatic power of this unseen force. *I'm powerless against the forces of darkness! You have rebuked Satan countless times before, and I ask that You do it again today!*

That was it—a very simple prayer, but one called up from the depths of Chen's heart and soul. It was all he had to offer. It was all he felt there was to say. God and Satan already knew the score in this woman's life. If the woman wanted to be delivered from the evil spirit, then God could and would do it. Chen was sure of that. The question was, When?

The family stood in the doorway of the room watching with bated breath. They knew Chen was a man of God and that his prayers to the God of heaven could work magic. But could he help their grandmother? Could he deliver her of the evil force now threatening to take her life?

Chen laid his hand on the little woman's forehead again and raised his eyes to heaven. "He who dwells in the secret place of the Most High shall abide under the shadow of the Almighty!" he said in a commanding tone. "Sister Yun, you have been held captive long enough! God is your Refuge and Fortress. In the name of Jesus, I ask that Satan torment you no more!"

There was a struggle in Yun's frail frame as the pain of her fever once again convulsed her body. She turned this way and that in great pain, and her eyes rolled back in their sockets. *Noooo!* she moaned, as if this might be her last hour on earth. Chen began reciting the words to the twenty-third psalm. "Even though I walk through the valley of the shadow of death I will fear no evil for You are with me." He was in enemy territory, and he knew the devil was not going to give up his victim without a fight. "Surely goodness and mercy shall follow me all the days of my life!"

The demon shook her one last time, and then she lay still, her body motionless. There was a long pause as the family watched intently to see what would happen next. Was Yun dead? Had the demon killed her? As the long moments passed and she still did not move, someone gasped. Chen could feel the pressure building as the family stared in silence, waiting impatiently to see the outcome of his prayer.

And then suddenly they saw Yun begin to breathe again more regularly, and everyone let out a sigh of relief as they, too, began to breathe normally.

Then her eyes opened and she smiled in surprised recognition of those standing near her bed. "Well, this is a fine place to find myself when guests are in the house! Has supper been started?" she exclaimed in embarrassment as she tried to sit up. "What's this young man doing here?" she added politely, looking at Chen. Some rushed forward to restrain her, but Chen took her by the hand and helped her to her feet.

"I think Sister Yun is fine now," he smiled. "And she's right. Let's get her something to eat. She hasn't eaten for several days now." It was truly a miracle of the highest order, and everyone standing in the room knew it.

As they all hurried around making preparations for the evening meal, Chen watched in enjoyment as this home was now released from the devil's power. No longer would Yun suffer from the pain of supernatural fevers. No longer would she hear the voices of the evil one whispering in her ear. She was free! As the family sat down to a meal of rice and stir-fried vegetables, they chattered excitedly, reciting the details again and again of how she had been delivered from Satan's power.

"Thank you! Thank you!" they all said as Chen finally left their house later that evening. They tried to pay him a few Chinese yuan for the good he had done in their home, but of course Chen would hear none of it. "This is not a time to be receiving money," Chen smiled and held up his hand in protest. "How can I take wages for something only God can give? Salvation is free, and the gift of God is eternal life."

"God is so good!" the family exclaimed when they saw this genuine display of kindness untouched by greed. "We never knew the prayer of a Christian could have such power until now! Praise God that His blessings have come to our house today!"

Chen was moved by the events of the day and bowed his head in humility as he left the house. The seeds of the gospel had been sowed once again for Jesus, this time in a dramatic miracle of healing. God had been glorified, and a little old woman had been released from the powers of darkness that had held her family captive for generations.

It was becoming clearer to Chen now why God had allowed the church board of Bible workers to be scattered in Shanghai. Perhaps this was God's way of bringing the light of truth to surrounding village communities like Wu Xi. As he walked up the little street to the home where he stayed, a verse of Scripture about the early Christian church came to mind, and the reality of it came to him like a ton of bricks on his soul.

"At that time a great persecution arose against the church which was at Jerusalem; and they were all scattered throughout the regions of Judea and Samaria. . . . Therefore those who were scattered went everywhere preaching the word" (Acts 8:1, 4, NKJV).

Chapter 11

In 1958, China's communist chairman, Mao Zedong, established a new government order called the Great Leap Forward. His new version of communism was shaking the culture of China like nothing anyone had seen before. The new plan earned him the unofficial title of Crazy Man because that's exactly what everyone was calling the sixty-four-year-old revolutionary.

Freedoms for towns and provinces to self-govern in any way were now eliminated almost completely. Factories that had been customarily assigning eight-hour work shifts were now given new orders—twelve- and fourteen-hour days. And for religious groups, the new regime's government controls were nightmarish. Mao's henchmen were now on a campaign warpath to control religious groups that were most active in evangelism and growth. And Christians were not the only ones Chairman Mao was cracking down on. All religious groups, including Buddhists and Muslims, were now being micromanaged.

Like the other religious groups, the Seventh-day Adventist church in Wu Xi had ceased to operate in a public way because of the government shutdown. Assembly for religious purposes was forbidden, so of course this made it impossible for Pastor Chen to worship with the Adventist believers in a church setting. All preaching and evangelistic crusades were outlawed. Only visitations to the homes of sick people were allowed, but it was no secret that even this was frowned upon by officials. And the reputation of Adventists was well-known. Of all Christians, it was said Adventists were "the most likely to proselytize."

Chen knew he must continue to minister to those in physical and spiritual need no matter the consequence. If there was a conflict between Chairman Mao and the God of all creation, Chen knew it didn't really matter what the state government was asking of him. He must represent his Maker. He must help spread the good news of the gospel. He must tell everyone who would listen that Jesus had lived and died for every sinner. With this attitude, he knew he would be prosecuted for his part in evangelism sooner or later. It couldn't be avoided.

Not if he was serious about fulfilling the commission Jesus had given every disciple who claimed His name.

It all came to a head one misty morning in June. The sun was just coming up over the rose-tinted horizon in the east, and songbirds had begun their predawn serenades. The vendors in the street were opening their shops, and a few children had already come out to play. The hills surrounding Wu Xi were beautiful this time of year, with rolling slopes of lavender and clover dotted here and there by grazing sheep.

Chen had finished his morning prayers and was now ready for a little exercise. There was nothing he enjoyed more than an early morning walk in the hills to start his day, but as he stepped out into the street, he was met by the village magistrate.

"You must stop your preaching in this village!" the magistrate barked without so much as a greeting. "A government inspector was here yesterday and has informed me they are watching you!"

Chen bowed politely but said nothing. It came as no shock that the government would be interested in what he was doing, but it did surprise him they had found him so quickly.

"You have been a good citizen, Mr. Chen," the magistrate softened his tone a bit, "and we appreciate all that you are doing for the sick and elderly among us. However, we must ask that you stop preaching and studying Christian books with your seven-day worshipers. Please, Mr. Chen," the magistrate gave him a pleading look. "Our town's reputation is on the line too. The government is watching you, but it is also watching us and is anxious to see that we cooperate with government officials in getting you to stop all such activities."

Chen bowed again. "I only wish to live in peace and serve my God," he said respectfully.

Beads of sweat jumped out on the magistrate's forehead as he frowned. "See that you do! Just don't let me hear you mentioning the name of your God!" he grumbled. "The last thing I need is for government officials to come prowling around looking for trouble!"

Things were getting serious, it appeared. Chen knew he had to be careful now if he valued his freedom, if he valued his life! Government officials would be watching him like a hawk from here on out. It was anybody's guess how hard they would be on those who caused them trouble. Pastor Lin and the other board members of the church in Shanghai had all been arrested and put in prison. Chen didn't know how they were doing, or if they were even free yet, but it wouldn't be much of a stretch to imagine himself in prison too.

He continued ministering to the elderly and the sick by visiting them in their homes. However, he knew he would have to change his strategy with the rest of the church members if he wanted to survive.

"We can't afford to meet like we have before," Chen announced to everyone as they all met to worship the next Sabbath morning in one of the homes. "From now on, we're going to have to meet early or late. No more meeting in broad daylight in places where people can see and hear us. This goes for Sabbath services or prayer meetings or early morning devotionals. If we don't do this, we'll all be at risk."

He glanced around the room at the few members present and wondered how much longer he could pull off this game of cat and mouse with government officials. It hadn't worked well in Shanghai, and he was now having his doubts about Wu Xi.

But Chen didn't have long to wonder. The very next Sabbath the magistrate knocked on the door at Jinhai's house where they were worshiping. "I see you've been at it again!" he scowled at Chen through the doorway. "Didn't I warn you folks about meeting like this? Your singing can be heard all up and down the street!"

He beckoned Chen through the open doorway to come outside. "You're going to bring a lot of unnecessary trouble for us here in Wu Xi, Mr. Chen, and I won't let you do it! For your disobedience, I am going to send you to live up on the mountain." He pointed to a small mountain overlooking the village of Wu Xi. It towered high above the village, and an old Buddhist temple capped its summit like a hat on a head. "The temple will be your new home," the magistrate added with a wave of his hand. "Our village has a flock of sheep up there. You can stay with them. That should slow you down a bit and make you behave yourself!"

"Yes, sir," Chen replied humbly. "How long must I stay?"

"Until you learn some manners and can take orders from your government." The magistrate turned to Chen again. "I have heard Christians speak of their preachers as shepherds. Is that not found in your Holy Book?" he smiled as if making a joke.

"It is so," Chen nodded, and he thought he knew where this conversation was going.

The magistrate began to chuckle to himself. "Then I will send you up to the mountain to be a real shepherd. You can preach to the sheep."

Chen collected his few belongings and said goodbye to his church family before making the short trip up the mountain road. By nightfall, he was settled in his new home. He knew the Buddhist temple had been shut down for some time now under the new communist government, but what he didn't know was that nine old monks were still living there. The government officials thought it was amusing to turn the old temple into a sheepfold, but Chen knew his real flock would be the Buddhist monks now. Already he could see his new role as an evangelist and realized how much potential there was for him here as a missionary to the monks.

"All things work together for good," Chen recounted the Bible promise to himself as he made himself a cup of tea that first night around a small, crackling fire (Romans 8:28, NKJV).

The monks were all old and infirm, and their heads were shorn bald. Their bright orange robes were colorful, but Chen never saw them change their clothing, and he guessed that in their poverty they owned only what they were wearing. They spent most of their time meditating as they chanted their prayers and sang the monotones of their holy dirges. Chen guessed most of them were over sixty years of age, and he couldn't help but feel sorry for them. The June evening was unusually cool, and as they all huddled under blankets on their sleeping mats that night, Chen could hear many of them coughing.

Chapter 12

Chen settled into his new life fulfilling his mission as shepherd of the monks. Unlike the monks, he was young and strong, and could do many of the everyday tasks necessary to make the temple their home. He collected wood and helped build the cooking fires. He helped sweep the temple floors every day, because Buddhists like to live in clean surroundings. When the red clay roof tiles shook loose during a rainstorm, he climbed up on the roof and replaced them.

The sheep needed to be taken to pasture and guarded against thieves and predators, so Chen went along to help. The monks milked the sheep and used this milk in their cooking, and Chen helped with that too. He had never milked a sheep before, or even tasted sheep's milk, but he soon grew used to both. Not surprisingly, he won his way into the hearts of the old monks.

But in those first few days with the monks, Chen learned a lot about their religion too. "There are Four Noble Truths," said Bohai, one of the oldest monks on the mountain. "Above all we wish above all to live by those truths," he told Chen one afternoon as the two of them were watching the sheep grazing on the mountain.

"Unfortunately, the world we live in is filled with *dukkhai,* the Buddhist word for anxiety and suffering," said Bohai. "Now, the greatest need of every Buddhist is to free himself from *dukkhai.* That's what the four great truths are all about: to help Buddhists find happiness and freedom from *dukkhai.* And, of course, we know the suffering in this world comes because humans look for happiness in all the wrong places," the old monk sighed.

"What about God?" Chen asked. "Doesn't He have a place in this world you call *dukkhai?*"

Bohai shook his head. "We do not believe that this world was created by one God as Christians do. For us, there are many gods. The goal of every good Buddhist is to live a good life and look for inspiration in the many heavenly buddhas, bodhisattvas, and deities that populate the universe. Our only hope is that they will help us."

"So you believe in many gods?" Chen picked a stem of grass and began to chew on it.

"That is correct."

"Do these gods always agree in the inspiration they give?"

"Not always."

"Then how do you know which one to listen to?"

"That is a difficult question, my son. We do the best we can."

"But doesn't that bring you more anxiety and suffering?"

"You ask hard questions," Bohai sighed. "We cannot know all things. Even Christians do not have all the answers to life."

"That is true," Chen nodded, "but the One True God whom I serve does know all the answers. In His Holy Book, He tells us where we came from, why we are here, and where we are going. He sent His only Son to this world to die for all the wrongs humans have ever done. If we confess the wrongs that we do personally, He will forgive us and make our lives clean and new again."

Bohai glanced at Chen skeptically. "And what must we do to receive this new life? Is there a shrine where we can burn incense to your God? Can we bring flowers or food or money?"

"There is nothing we can do to receive this gift except surrender our lives and hearts in service to the God of heaven," Chen replied. "We cannot pay for it with silver or incense or flowers. We cannot do enough good deeds to receive it, nor is there any deed so bad that it will keep us from getting it," Chen added. "If we confess our wrongs, He is faithful to forgive us and will cleanse us from all that would defile us in this world."

Bohai stared down at the valley below them. "I did not know all this about your God. If He does all this, He must truly be an amazing Deity."

There was a long pause as Chen prayed for the right words to say. "Honorable Bohai, are you happy with the path your life has taken?"

"I have done the best I can with what I have been taught," Bohai replied. "Buddha has told us that life is a journey. Death is a return to earth, and the passing years are like dust. The universe is like an inn. We must regard this world we live in as a star at dawn, a bubble in a stream. It is like a flash of lightning in a summer cloud, a flickering lamp, a phantom, and a dream. What more can a man do?" Bohai raised his eyebrows at Chen. "Is there more?"

Chen smiled reassuringly. "The God of heaven tells us there is more, my friend. Much more. If you have lived with the fear and anxiety all men experience in this world, then I have good news for you. In His Holy Book, my God explains why there is suffering. Bad things do happen to good people. We cannot always escape suffering in this world, but He has promised us that if we listen to His voice and obey His commands, we can one day escape this old world and its suffering. One day soon God will come to take us away to live with Him forever in His heavenly home."

An afternoon breeze blew across the grassy slopes of the mountain, rustling the orange folds of the old monk's robes. He glanced up at the balmy skies of blue, his gray eyes perhaps searching to catch a glimpse of this God Chen spoke of somewhere in the heavens.

"I thank you for telling me about your God," Bohai smiled weakly. "I think I could believe in your God if He is everything you say He is."

"My God is your God because He created you, Bohai," Chen put his hands together and bowed in the Buddhist way. "And the best part is that He never changes. Not ever. He is the same yesterday, today, and forever. That makes Him even more wonderful because you know you can count on Him to stay the same and keep His Word as He has promised."

Chen guessed he would be living on the mountain for a while, but he couldn't help wondering how his little church flock was doing down in the village. Were they worshiping together for Sabbath services? Were they meeting in one another's homes for prayer meeting? Who was tending the sick and elderly? Were they praying for him up on this mountain while he was praying for them down in the valley?

Every day, two or three of the monks would go down to the market to beg for rice with their sacred pots and then buy the vegetables they needed for their meals on the mountain. They also took their surplus supply of sheep's milk to be bartered in the market for other things they might need.

One morning, Chen offered to go with them to help carry the cans of milk and bring vegetables back up the mountain. What harm would it do? The magistrate wouldn't mind. And besides, Chen felt he deserved a nice walk after being cooped up in the old temple on the mountain. And who knew, by chance he might even be lucky enough to see some of his church members in the village market.

The old monks took their time picking out the spinach, cabbage, and onions at the vegetable market vendors, and while they were there, Chen glanced over the crowded heads in the marketplace. Sure enough, his benefactor, Mrs. Liu, was there along with old Mrs. Yun, the woman he had helped release from demon possession.

Chen exchanged simple greetings with these women because he didn't want to give the town magistrate reasons for suspicion; then he headed back up the mountain with the monks and their load of vegetables. However, Chen thought about that first visit to the village and decided he would go again the next chance he got.

On his next trip into the village, he met the magistrate in the market again and the two of them had a pleasant conversation. That simple gesture emboldened Chen, and he decided he would sneak down into the village the next Sabbath to attend church with his fellow believers. For several weeks, he managed to meet with the brothers and sisters, and wisely enough they did not sing songs during their worship together.

However, one afternoon when he was leaving the home of an elderly man in the village, he once again chanced to meet the magistrate in the street. "I see you are coming down to the village again regularly," the wily official retorted.

"Yes, sir," Chen bowed his head in the customary fashion. "I was under the impression that you were thinking more favorably of me now."

"Is that so?" the magistrate studied Chen's face. "Very well then, you may come down to the village on business, but don't let me catch you coming down for worship services on Saturdays." He noticed the surprised look on Chen's face. "I'm no fool," he added. "My informants tell me you've been coming down to worship with your seven-day group for several weeks now."

Chen half smiled and kept his eyes on the ground. "Does that mean I can't visit the sick in their homes?"

"I'm saying no such thing. I'm simply asking that you stop meeting with your church group to preach." The magistrate shrugged. "Let's be perfectly clear, young man. Stay on the mountain every Saturday, and I'll consider us friends."

Chapter 13

Chen decided it would be wise to follow the magistrate's warning for a time at least, even if it meant the church group would be shortchanged, even if he could have justified himself in the name of Jesus for obvious evangelistic reasons. And so he sent word to Jinhai that, regrettably, he was again being confined to his mountain home, but he would pray for them from his temple retreat. What else could he do?

But shortly after dawn that first Sabbath away from his flock, Chen was pleasantly surprised when Jinhai and Liu showed up at the mountain temple. Liu's mother, Shihong, was also with them. "What brings you to the mountain?" Chen asked, his eyes lighting up with delight at the sight of his good friends.

"We were discouraged when we heard that the town magistrate had forbidden you from worshiping with us," Jinhai announced. "However, this morning while Liu was on her knees praying, she felt impressed that there was something we could do to help." His wrinkled old face broke into a humble grin. "If you cannot go to us in the village, we must come to you on the mountain."

"Marvelous! What a wonderful surprise!" Chen's eyes misted over at these words of encouragement. "May God bless you for your kindness to me," he said, "and for your faithfulness in doing what I could not do. You have made my day like nothing else could!"

"You are not an ordinary man," Jinhai winked at Chen. "That is why the communist leaders know they must keep tabs on you and follow you around. They know you are a man of God who brings the power of heaven to our village when you share the gospel story." He pointed to heaven. "That is why they spy on you as you work," he added. "And that is why we must support you as our pastor. We need you. Wu Xi needs you, and we must help you win many hearts to Jesus in our village."

Chen was cheered by the love and devotion of these good folks. With such a simple faith among God's people, how could the gospel not grow and prosper in Wu Xi?

The Adventist believers in Wu Xi continued to come to the old Buddhist temple on the mountain for several weeks. It seemed that this was the answer to their problems with the communist government controls on their pastor and their church, and Chen couldn't help but smile. He and his church members were meeting secretly on the mountain to avoid detection by the town magistrate, and they were doing it in an abandoned Buddhist temple. Could there be a stranger set of circumstances in all of China? Surely God had a sense of humor!

By now, life had settled into a routine for Chen, and he was even beginning to thank God for his temple home on the mountain. And when Brother Wencheng, a member of his church group, gave him an old bicycle, Chen felt even more blessed.

"Now you won't have to walk up and down the mountain road carrying that heavy can of milk anymore," the elderly church member said. "And you can put your vegetables in the basket on the handlebars for the ride back up the mountain too."

"You are so kind to think of me," Chen smiled at his kind benefactor. "God has given me such good friends."

In the days that followed, the bike indeed turned out to be a blessing for everyone, including the monks. Now they no longer had to go to the market because Chen could easily transport the milk, rice, and vegetables himself.

The long hot days of summer passed, and before Chen knew it, the shorter, cooler ones of fall had arrived. The grass was shorter and browner on the hills surrounding Wu Xi now. Summer was not as bright, though violets, hibiscus, and peonies still decorated the roadsides and lanes leading into town. The little lambs in the flock on the mountain had grown big and fat, and the fields of rice in the boggy lowlands had long since been harvested and threshed out by the village winnowers.

Near the end of September, Chen was invited to conduct the marriage of two young Adventist members in Wu Xi. "There is no one who can conduct the wedding for us because there is no other Christian pastor in town," Liko, the groom, said earnestly. "Zongying and I request that you perform the ceremony for us at my father's house, and we would be honored if you could stay for the reception too."

And so Chen came down off the mountain and celebrated the special day with Liko and Zongying, the young couple to be married. It was a very traditional wedding with friends and family since it was an arranged marriage. Red was the color of choice splashed everywhere, from flowers to decorations to Zongying's wedding dress. A traditional circular double-happiness symbol hung over the couple's wedding table, and the tea ceremony was unforgettable.

The wedding feast was loaded with foods that symbolized long life and prosperity. As was customary, eight courses were served, since eight was thought to be a lucky number. Vegetables were served with many rice dishes, and there were all kinds of fresh fruits and soups to whet the appetites of the wedding guests. The main courses for Chinese weddings usually featured duck or goose, but Chen had instructed the couple that such meat was unfit for food according to the Bible, so they served chicken instead.

Even so, the types of dishes served were quite simple. The previous summer had been a bad one for many regions in eastern China because of floods, so the wedding family did the best they could with what they could find in the markets.

What a special day, Chen thought to himself as he lay down to sleep that night on his reed mat in the Buddhist temple. What a wonderful day to celebrate the beginning of a new life for a young couple that was dedicating their home to God!

That was September 26 of 1960, and Chen had no idea how much the wedding event would change his life in the months to come. If he had, he might have turned down the request to conduct the wedding. Then again, maybe he wouldn't have. After all, marriage was one of the most sacred gifts from God, the most special of ceremonies tying earth to heaven.

One bright morning a few days later, a stranger in uniform stopped Chen as he came into town on his bicycle. "Don't bring your milk to the market today," he said sternly. "Go back up the mountain."

Chen looked at the official in surprise. "What's the problem, officer?" The man was clearly someone important by the look of his uniform, and Chen guessed he was a government official of some kind.

"No problem," the official retorted, but the tone in his voice told Chen that trouble indeed was coming. "Go tell all the monks that I want to have a meeting with them at the temple later this morning."

Chen turned his bike around and rode it back up the mountain as he had been told. The incline up the mountain trail was steep, and with a full can of milk, he had to pedal hard to make the strenuous grade. The sweat poured from his body drenching his shirt, and every turn of the pedals seemed to be saying, "Trouble, trouble, trouble!"

When he arrived at the temple, old Bohai was sitting alone in a stance of meditation. Chen's heart was hammering away in his chest from the long ride up the hill. He didn't want to disturb his Buddhist friend as he stood to the side silently waiting for Bohai to finish. The old man was sitting so still that Chen almost had to smile. He could never tell for sure if these monks were breathing or even alive.

After several long moments, Bohai finally took a long breath and then turned to Chen. "What is it, my son? Your face looks troubled."

"We're going to have visitors," Chen announced. "A government official is on his way up the mountain to speak to us. He wants to meet with all of us here at the temple."

"And you're thinking this is a bad thing?" Bohai's eyebrows lifted.

Chen hung his head. "I think it's because of me that they are coming." A look of sadness and disappointment settled on his face.

"It is the will of the gods," the old monk murmured. "For each of us there must be burdens to bear in this life. For each there must be some suffering that will make us into better people."

Chen realized this might be the last time he would have a chance to speak to Bohai about the God of heaven and His love for the human race. He must say something special that would stay in Bohai's mind, something to help Bohai understand the love of the Father for him personally.

Chapter 14

hen settled himself on a mat beside Bohai sitting in the Buddhist fashion. "God created you in His own image, Bohai. He loves you so much that He sent His only Son Jesus to suffer and die in this world so you could have eternal life with Him." Chen's voice was earnest with conviction as he folded his hands under his nose in prayerful respect. "Every day He sends angels to watch over you to keep you from harm. Soon He will come to take us from this world to be with Him where He is."

Bohai lifted his hands in response to Chen. "Thank you for those kind words of comfort, young man. You are like a son to me." He bowed his head reverently. "Will you teach me to pray to the God of heaven?"

And so they prayed together. Both with heads bowed. Both sitting cross-legged on mats laid on the temple floor where tens of thousands before them had prayed to Buddha. Both felt the power of God in this pagan shrine to the power of Satan. Chen asked that the Spirit of God would give Bohai peace by cleansing him of every sin.

And to Bohai, the effect was quite magical. He was now strangely aware that the God of heaven was very near. The gods of gold and jade and marble he had always served would not save him—could not save him—from his life of aimless pain and suffering. They could no more bring him heaven's salvation than the ants crawling back and forth across the ornate tiles on the temple floor.

And then the moment was over, and Chen could hear the crunch of gravel on the pathway leading up the mountain to the temple. Three military police had arrived, and with them, a warrant for Chen's arrest and a summons for him to return with them back down the mountain. There would be no meeting with the monks as he had been told. They had deceived him and lied about their true intentions for the meeting.

But Chen knew he shouldn't really be surprised. Did any of this really make a difference? This was the way of ungodly men. And besides, God had other things for him to do now elsewhere in His great vineyard. Chen had shared these few weeks with the monks. He had brought them words of peace and hope and life, and now it was time for him to move on.

"The village magistrate told us why he sent you up here on the mountain!" growled one of the police. "He meant to keep you from spreading the poison of your religion, but it appears his words have fallen on deaf ears." Roughly, the police shackled Chen's hands behind him in a pair of handcuffs. There was no real need for such force, Chen thought, but obviously the police didn't agree.

"We've been watching you!" the officer checked the cuffs and gave them a painful yank for good measure. "Not only have you been worshiping with your seven-day Advent members each Saturday up here on the mountain, you're now infecting the monks who live in the temple." The police officer gestured wildly toward the monks who had gathered to watch from the adjoining wings of the temple.

"I mean no harm," Chen replied quietly. "I only wish to tell the story of Jesus and how He came to save mankind from a life of suffering in this world."

"Well, you are causing harm!" argued the officer. "How can our country make the great leap forward when it has to continually battle the likes of you? You're a parasite! You Christians are like a disease that can't be stopped!" He spat the words out as if they had left a bad taste in his mouth. "Get him out of here!" He jerked his head toward the village at the base of the mountain.

A military policeman (MP) pushed Chen toward the mountain trail. "We're going to cure you of this nonsense!" he snickered. "When we're done with you, all the notions of this crazy religion will be out of your head!"

What could Chen say? They were right! He was crazy! His head was full of notions about salvation from Jesus, loving his fellow men, and a peace that defies all understanding. But the best part of it was that God had put the ideas there.

Chen could not explain why he must share the story of salvation with anyone and everyone who would listen! There was no good earthly explanation for the fire that filled his veins to preach the gospel! He could see why his stubborn devotion to God would drive the police insane with anger. It was not logical. It was not rational, and it was certainly not compatible with what the new communist government was trying to do. Ridding China of its superstitious traditions and irrational beliefs, whether they were Christian, Buddhist or Muslim, made perfect sense to people who didn't know the Living God, the Sovereign of eternity, time, and space.

But Chen did know the Living God. The Seventh-day Adventist believers in the village knew God and worshiped Him. And now, Bohai knew this God of heaven who had come that all men might have life and that they might have it more abundantly. How could one keep silent about such a thing? How could one conceal the best news the world has ever known?

Chen walked with his head high as the four of them descended the mountain trail to the village. He didn't know what was coming next, but prison for him was the most likely scenario. That was really no surprise. For Chen, it had always been just a matter of time before he ended up in prison. Thousands of brothers and sisters in China had suffered imprisonment and even death for spreading the gospel, so why should he be any different? Why should he be an exception? Why should he receive better treatment than his fellow servants and even Jesus himself? *If they were unjustly treated, why not me?* Chen told himself. *It is an honor beyond all honors to suffer for the cause of Christ.*

When the group reached the town market, they all got into a jeep. The jeep lurched forward and then began careening through the alleys and streets of Wu Xi until it came to the local jail. Without warning, it screeched to a stop, catapulting Chen forward almost into the front seat. One of the MPs pulled Chen from the jeep, his hands still cuffed behind his back. Before he could catch himself, Chen fell heavily, face down in the dirty street, but the MP showed no sympathy.

"Get up, dog!" he shouted, jerking Chen to his feet. He shoved Chen along impatiently toward the prison gate. "Stop fooling around! We don't have time to waste!"

As they hurried through the prison gate and down a darkened corridor, Chen sized up the frightening surroundings. Everything looked broken down and dilapidated—the doors, the walls, the holding cells—and the stench in the place was awful, as if death itself were there! And what did he expect? He was in a prison. He had heard about places like this, but had never been in one before.

Please Lord, he prayed, *help me to be brave and courageous for You no matter what happens while I'm here! Like me, Jesus was despised and rejected when He was in this world. He was a Man of sorrows and acquainted with grief. He was bruised for my iniquities. He was oppressed and afflicted for me personally, yet He didn't complain. How can I do less for Him?* (see Isaiah 53). A peace settled down upon Chen, and suddenly he knew he would be all right. God was with him in this place.

They turned down another corridor and came to an open space with several large jail cells surrounding it. The MPs released Chen to the jailer and then turned to go. "Enjoy your new home!" they hooted, and Chen could hear them laughing all the way back down the corridor.

A guard led Chen to one of the large cells. He opened the lock on cell number four and pushed Chen inside. "There you are!" the guard announced loudly. "This is your worst nightmare! Cell number four! Bad luck in anybody's book, I'd say!" he laughed wickedly. "That will keep you on your toes!"

What a beginning, thought Chen. Everyone in China was superstitiously afraid of the number four, in any form, especially when it was associated with something that was already bad. But Chen paid the number no mind. That was the least of his worries. When a man serves the God of the universe, no number or symbol is bad luck. God is in control of all things.

"You can take that spot right there," the guard pointed to an empty mat near the cell door. "It's the only one left." He stared at Chen with an almost comical look on his face. "What crime did you commit, holy man?" he jeered. "Must have been pretty bad to put you in here with all these barbarians."

Chen shrugged. "I don't really know. I've broken no laws of community living." He paused. "They want me to stop telling others about the God of heaven, that much I can say, but I can't in good conscience do that. If Jesus died to give you and me eternal life, the least we can do is tell everyone about the good news. For God's sake, I am glad to do it, even if it lands me in a place like this."

The jailer clanged the cell door behind Chen and shook his head in disbelief. He had never heard any prisoner give such a testimony. Most had feigned ignorance of the crimes they had committed, protesting their incarceration and abuse, but few took their sentence so willingly without complaining. "You're a strange one," he exclaimed through the prison bars. "I've seen many criminals in my day but none who were ignorant of their crime and still had such peace."

Chapter 15

Chen's eyes opened wide as he entered his prison cell. He could not believe the conditions of his new living quarters. Dozens of prisoners were crammed into a space not more than six meters long and four meters wide. Everywhere covering every square inch of the floor were crusty straw sleeping mats lined up in rows and filthy, bug-infested blankets thrown in little rumpled piles along the wall.

But the smell of the place shocked his senses the most. Near the gate of the prison cell was a gutter with a drain and a chamber pot. That was the bathroom for the prisoners, and the stench that permeated the place was almost unbearable! Flies buzzed everywhere, and Chen knew they would be his greatest enemy as transmitters of disease. Evidently, the cool evenings hadn't chased them away yet. He didn't want to think what the fly population might look like during the hot summer months. What an experience this was going to be! He had suffered under harsh conditions before, but this was unthinkable! In this place, men were forced to live in an environment that was anything but human, and nobody in the outside world even knew about it.

Chen glanced around quickly at the motley group and counted over forty inmates. His heart beat faster at the scene before him. Prisoners of every description sat or lay on the sleeping mats. Were they all criminals, or were some imprisoned here, like him, on trumped-up charges? Some of them looked friendly enough, though one could never tell what a fellow prisoner might turn out to be in a place like this. Others looked like emaciated skeletons, as if they hadn't eaten in weeks. He guessed these men had probably been in prison the longest.

But the evil, mean-looking ones worried Chen the most. Were they hardened, vicious felons capable of committing heinous crimes? Would they beat him or rob him? He didn't have anything of value on him, but they might not know that. Chen supposed there were worse things they could do if they got angry, and the thought that they might be capable of murder sent shivers down his spine.

He sat down on his mat and glanced around warily at the other prisoners. What would happen to him here? He could feel them all watching him, and he didn't dare close his eyes for fear of what they might do to him. *Dear Lord, please help me!* he prayed desperately. *I have tried to be faithful, to be a witness for You wherever You have asked me to go, but this is different! I'm in a prison now, and I'm scared, Lord! I don't know what to expect. Help me know what to do.*

Suddenly, into his mind came well-known verses of Scripture he had memorized, clearly for just such a time as this. *"Save me, O God, by your name; vindicate me by your might. Hear my prayer, O God; listen to the words of my mouth. Arrogant foes are attacking me; ruthless people are trying to kill me—people without regard for God. Surely God is my help. The Lord is the one who sustains me"* (Psalm 54:1–4, NIV).

The verses were like a tonic calming his nerves, and before long he was himself again. He was going to be all right. Whatever happened here was part of God's plan for him. If they robbed him or mistreated him, God knew about it and was watching over him. If they beat him, Jesus had suffered such things before.

Chen now noticed other things about the prison too. His cell was lined with bars along the sides and top. Prisoners lived on the ground floor, and the guards walked on a catwalk above the cell. Far above them was a tin roof to protect the prisoners from sun and rain. That was a blessing, but Chen also noticed gaps in the walls along the roof. He shivered at the thought of cold rain and snow blowing in through those gaps. Such a thing didn't seem to be much of a problem in late September, but come winter he knew it would be unthinkably cold.

But the strangest thing of all was the fact that no one in the prison was talking. Other than the guards calling to one another from here and there in the prison complex, no one spoke a word in Chen's cell or in any of the other prison cells for that matter. He thought that was odd. What was wrong? Had they been in here so long they had forgotten how to talk? Were they just bored, or had they maybe run out of things to say? Or was it something else? Chen didn't know, but he had to find out.

He glanced at the prisoner sitting on the mat next to him. The man was of small build and didn't look too scary. Chen considered himself a good judge of character on first sight, and he figured he could take a chance with this one. The man's balding shock of gray-black hair made him look old, but then maybe everyone looked old after living for a while in a place like this. Strangely enough, the man's eyes drew Chen to him most. They appeared vacant and lost, as if the prisoner hadn't a friend in the world who cared whether he lived or died.

Chains in China

"What's your name?" Chen whispered, looking at him out of the corner of his eye.

The prisoner frowned and turned away from Chen as if to ignore him. "Huang Fu," he said under his breath.

Chen nodded slowly. "How long have you been here?" he added, hoping to continue the conversation and make a friend.

"Six months," Huang Fu whispered back and frowned again, staring straight forward.

Chen glanced around at the other prisoners naïvely. "Why is everyone so quiet in here?" he added.

Huang Fu gave Chen a dirty look and glanced at the jailer sitting in a chair outside the cell. "The guards don't like us talking to each other. It's against the rules!" he hissed. "You want to get us both in trouble?"

Chen gulped and stared forward now. He, too, hoped to avoid trouble with the guards for talking. How was he to know the rules in this prison? He had only wanted to be friendly to a fellow prisoner. No one had bothered to tell him what was allowed and what wasn't. Not the guards. Not even the warden. Chen guessed he was going to have to find out things the hard way. In a place like this, was there any other option?

"Watch your step, preacher man!" Huang Fu gave Chen one final warning and glanced in the other direction again. "Whatever they tell you to do, just do it, or you'll be in here forever!"

The words sounded ominous, and Chen felt a growing tightness in his chest at the warning. Maybe he had been wrong about Huang Fu. Maybe Huang Fu was a desperate criminal who would kill him while he slept.

But something about the man had made Chen want to continue the conversation. He had called Chen "preacher man." How did he know Chen was a preacher? Had Chen's reputation already filtered through the social network of the prison? Was it something the guard said about him beeing a holy man that tipped off Huang Fu?

Please Lord, Chen prayed again. *Help me to make a difference in this place, beginning with Huang Fu. I'm not a troublemaker, Lord. Help me to bring words of life to all these prisoners, and help me to stay out of trouble. You're my only hope.*

Chen glanced around at his surroundings again: the sights, the sounds, the men. He studied the bars along the sides and top of the prison cell and noticed how much the place looked like a cage. It was a strange sensation, and the more he thought about it, the more he felt like an animal cooped up against its will. What an awful feeling!

He remembered catching a little rabbit once when he was a boy. He had built a cage for the rabbit and gathered all kinds of plants for it, but the little creature wouldn't eat. He had wanted to keep the rabbit as a pet, but it had gotten sick and died. Now he understood why. He had taken away the most precious thing the rabbit had—its freedom.

For the first time in his life, Chen felt he understood the true meaning of freedom. In this prison, he was very much like an animal—that little rabbit, maybe, or one of the lions or bears he had seen in the Shanghai zoo. He had always felt sympathy for such animals, but those days were gone. Now he had little time to feel bad for them, or anyone else for that matter. Mostly, he was feeling bad for himself.

As the hours passed with nothing to do but sit, Chen found himself growing more and more discouraged. What was he to do with all his time? How would he keep his sanity with no one to talk to and nothing to do? And then, suddenly, a whistle sounded from somewhere in the prison. In an instant, the place came alive with prisoners, jostling and shoving each other as they scrambled to get a place in line. *That has to be the signal for the evening meal,* Chen thought.

Chapter 16

Chen was last in line to get his rations, but he didn't care. He wasn't hungry anyway. Everything about the prison made him nauseous, and eating was the last thing on his mind. The guards were dishing out metal cups of watery gruel for the prisoners to eat, and by the way the prisoners gulped the stuff, it couldn't be all bad. But Chen was suspicious of the gruel. It had a few sickly-looking pieces of carrots and potato floating on top, and it didn't look appetizing to him at all.

"It's corn porridge," Huang Fu whispered when he saw Chen staring into the cup. "It's a bit salty, but you'll get used to it. You'll have to sooner or later because we eat this stuff three times a day."

Three times a day! Chen made a face at the thought of such a thing. He took a whiff of the gruel and jerked his head back at its sickening odor. The watery porridge was downright disgusting! How could he eat it? It looked bad and smelled bad, and he didn't even want to think about the despicable things that might be in it!

As a boy growing up, he had eaten a lot of cornmeal mush, but this didn't look much like corn. It was more gray-green than yellow. He knew he should have been hungry, and he knew he needed to keep up his strength for what might be coming, but he just couldn't bring himself to eat the nasty stuff. It wasn't even hot. The cup was already cold in his hands, if it had ever been warm.

"Here," Chen extended the cup of gruel to his new friend. "You can have mine."

His cellmate took one look at Chen, and then snatched the cup from his hands. "Thanks," he grunted as he noisily slurped the corn gruel, and within seconds, it was gone.

That night as Chen lay on his moldy old sleeping mat, he struggled with the reality of his situation. A feeble lightbulb burning somewhere above him threatened to keep him awake. Instinctively, he squeezed his eyes shut to block out the light and to keep himself from remembering the depravity of his surroundings. But that didn't keep him from smelling the tide of ghastly odors now overpowering his senses. And it didn't keep him from hearing the grunts and groans of the men as they settled in for a long night on the cold stone floor.

God is my refuge and strength, he kept reminding himself bravely. *Jesus will not forsake me. Though the wicked should surround me and hedge me in, the angels will guard me while I sleep. Though I am shut up in prison, the Holy Spirit will give me the strength and courage to be a man for God.*

He didn't think he was going to be able to sleep on a hard floor in a place crawling with germs and vermin, but to his surprise, he felt himself growing sleepy. Maybe he was more tired than he had thought. And if the mat on which he was lying hadn't been so despicably rank with the smell of urine, he might almost have smiled. *God has a strange way of prepping the mind for circumstances that are less than ideal,* he thought. "I must be a soldier for God," he whispered into the darkness, and then drifted off to sleep.

Chen awoke the next morning with a wonderful feeling of peace, but when he remembered where he was, the old feelings of despair returned. He tried to fight it, but the sensation that he was abandoned and alone and forgotten by God was almost more than he could bear.

Was it possible that only a few days before he had been at the marriage banquet? It had been such a pleasant day with the wedding couple celebrating their happy new life together. Wonderful, supportive church members had been gathered for the occasion. The colors of red and white were still so vivid in Chen's mind, and the food had been sensational. The thought of such bliss was a wonderful memory, but thinking about it now was too torturous, and it threatened to overwhelm him emotionally. The contrast between that pleasure and this pain was too great!

Here he was in this prison, an appalling place of evil and disease, full of decrepit prisoners and heartless prison officials. He had no soap to clean himself, if it mattered. They were not allowed to take baths or showers anyway. He had not been given an opportunity to bring anything with him from his temple room up on the mountain—no razor to shave himself, no toothbrush to clean his teeth, not even a change of clothing to help him start each day right. His dignity was suffering and his freedom was gone in exchange for a life of abuse and poor food.

And that's exactly where Chen's day now started. With poor food, if one could call it food. For breakfast, the prisoners were given the same porridge, but again Chen couldn't bring himself to eat any of it. He just couldn't stomach the idea of eating the cold, slimy gruel everyone was calling corn porridge. The very thought of it made him ill, and he hadn't even tasted it yet. The smell was enough to make him retch. How was he ever going to get up the courage to taste the corn gruel, let alone eat it three times a day!

Chen didn't want to think about that. It was hard enough being in prison, let alone not being able to look forward to meals. Why couldn't he get past this proverbial bump in the road? Food was food, if it kept you alive. Was he too good to eat the food the prisoners were given? There was no meat in the stewlike porridge, that much was sure. He had dared to ask Huang Fu about that before breakfast. Likely, the prison officials couldn't afford the price of meat on their prison budget.

"Meat, in the porridge?" Huang Fu had whispered, his eyes laughing almost hysterically. "In this prison? I wish! They never give us meat unless it's a special holiday!"

That put Chen's mind at ease a bit but not enough yet to make him eat the cold gruel. Sooner or later, he knew he was going to have to get off his high horse and try some of the porridge, but when that would be, he couldn't say. For now, eating anything in this place was still on hold. It looked like fasting would be his best friend. That was a concept for the memory books! If his situation hadn't been so serious, he might have even smiled.

After breakfast, everyone went back to their sleeping mats and lay down or sat cross-legged on the floor. The space in the jail cell was too small to do anything else. Chen felt bad for the prisoners as he watched them in their boredom. As Huang Fu had said, the guards forbade the men from talking among themselves. They couldn't exercise, they couldn't walk around, and there were no books for them to read. There was virtually nothing for them to do.

And he felt bad for himself. After all, he was a prisoner too. The lunacy of it all threatened to overwhelm him, so he tried to stop thinking about it.

Under these conditions, the prison remained painfully quiet. All Chen could hear were the guards talking among themselves, their footsteps echoing down the corridors, or the clatter of nightsticks being dragged along the iron bars of the prison cells. At first, this was all very depressing for Chen, but then he grew accustomed to it and made a wonderful, startling discovery. The revelation came to him that prison might be an ideal place for prayer and meditation. The serenity of the place might serve him well, if one could think of serenity and this prison cell in the same breath.

Chapter 17

Chen decided to put his new philosophy into practice immediately. What better way was there to spend his time than in prayer? The living conditions in this prison were a disaster, but the angels of heaven were here to help him get through it. The Holy Spirit was here giving him courage and strength and peace. Chen bowed his head and began to think of Scripture verses that would be inspirational. Anything right now would be a help.

"Do not be anxious about anything." Those words seemed to hit the spot perfectly. He closed his eyes and began reciting passages from Philippians, chapter 4. *"In every situation, by prayer and petition, with thanksgiving, present your requests to God. And the peace of God, which transcends all understanding, will guard your hearts and your minds in Christ Jesus"* (verses 6, 7, NIV).

Now that was a verse! Down through the years as a young man, he had spent much of his time studying the Bible, and one of his favorite things to do was memorize Bible verses. His father had told him that true Christians should put much of the Bible to memory to be used in times of temptation, trial, and persecution. "It may be the only thing you have some day if you are in prison," he had said. Chen could not believe how true those words had become, and he was so very glad now that he had taken his father's advice.

Chen was so inspired by the passage from Philippians that he decided to write it down on a little piece of paper he found lying on the floor. That way, he could read it any time he wanted to encourage himself. He rummaged in his shirt pocket and found a short stub of pencil to write the verse. The pencil was one of the few things he had managed to bring with him to the prison, and he was excited at his good fortune of having it. What a blessing!

Remembering verses to recite and then write was especially helpful because it gave Chen something to do to keep his mind occupied. Right now that seemed like a good idea. He had read about prisoners who went crazy from the torture of boredom, and he didn't want that to happen to him.

Every time he got the pencil out, he checked to see if the guards were watching. The last thing he wanted was for them to come and take his pencil away. He tried to write the Chinese characters small so the pencil (and the piece of paper) would last longer. Then he thought of other verses and wrote them on the paper. When he had filled up one side of the paper, he turned it over and wrote on the other side as well. Some verses came easier than others, but the little task was always an inspirational one. As each verse came to mind, Chen could feel the Holy Spirit upon him, bringing him the verses he needed most for a time like this. It was as if the power of God had come to dwell with him in the prison cell.

The biggest question in his mind now was where to keep the piece of paper with the Bible verses on it. That was a difficult dilemma. Inside his clothing? In the small pillow he slept on? Sewed up in a blanket? Keeping the paper hidden was probably the best thing to do since it did have Bible verses written on it, something the guards might consider contraband. Contraband would be anything that a prisoner might have in his possession that was forbidden. Drugs would be in that category, as would political propaganda materials. Anything religious might also get him into trouble since all religions were said to be at war with the philosophy of Mao Zedong's Great Leap Forward. Under the dictator's new regime, religion was considered political poison because it made people "think irrationally and superstitiously." All religions were now declared to be unscientific, outmoded forms of thinking, and relics of the ignorant past.

After much thought, Chen realized there was really no safe place to conceal the scrap of paper from the watchful eyes of the guards. Even worse, he could never really trust his fellow prisoners to keep such a thing secret. It would seem that the prisoners would highly value sticking together and supporting one another, but, evidently, that was not the case. He had heard of prisoners turning in their fellow inmates just to get an extra cup of porridge or maybe a chance to stretch their legs outside the jail cell.

After much thought, Chen finally tucked the scrap of paper with Bible verses inside the lining of the old pillow the prison officials had given him. That would keep it secure and ready to read again whenever he felt he needed it.

What a blessing the Scriptures were to him! He closed his eyes and repeated the verse from Philippians 4 once again. *"In every situation, by prayer and petition, with thanksgiving, present your requests to God. And the peace of God, which transcends all understanding, will guard your hearts and your minds in Christ Jesus."*

"Prisoner, what are you doing!" Chen suddenly heard a voice shouting and opened his eyes to see a guard staring through the bars in his direction.

Chen blinked in confusion at the sight of the guard. Was he shouting at Chen or someone else? The prisoners were packed into the jail cell so tightly, it was hard to tell.

"Yes, you!" the guard pointed his nightstick at Chen angrily. "I'm talking to you! Are you deaf?"

"*Um,* no, sir!" Chen stammered in surprise. His mind raced to think what the problem might be. What had he done? Had the officer seen him writing the Bible verses and then tucking the paper inside his pillow?

"Answer the question," the guard glared at him. "I asked you, 'What you are doing?' "

"Uh, doing, sir? I wasn't doing anything. Was I, sir?" Chen's mind raced to think of what to do. If the Bible verses had made the guard angry, he knew he was in trouble. Or had he done anything at all? Was the officer maybe just pestering him, trying to make his life miserable? Wasn't that what life was all about in this prison? Chen would have liked to think out loud here and tell the prison guard exactly what he was thinking, but, of course, he knew that would be a stupid and suicidal move for sure.

He finally shrugged. "I must have done something to make you angry, sir, but I don't know what it is."

"Don't get smart with me!" the guard shouted, extending his nightstick through the bars of the cell to point it at Chen. "You had your eyes shut, prisoner! Why?" Chen had to lean back to keep from being poked with the nightstick.

So that was it. The guard had seen him with his eyes closed. Did he think Chen had been sleeping? Was sleeping not allowed during the day? Chen had seen plenty of others dozing where they sat or lay on their sleeping mats. Was that against the rules too?

And then the reality of the moment hit Chen. He had been praying. The guard had seen him with eyes closed and lips moving, but was that what he was upset about? Could he tell Chen had been praying?

Chapter 18

Chen stared at the guard. "Sir, I was praying," he admitted.

"That's what I thought you were doing," the guard growled, "and it's not allowed in here!"

"No praying?" Chen mouthed the words silently and glanced around him at the other prisoners, but none of them were looking at him. "I'm not allowed to pray?" he asked out loud.

"Pray to what?" the guard sneered. "There is no God! The honorable Mao Zedong has taught us that much in his Great Leap Forward! So then, who are you praying to?" He raised his eyebrows. "No one, I tell you! Your God exists only in your mind, and we don't allow such nonsense in here!" he snorted. "It's not good for prison morale!"

Chen was tongue-tied. How could these prison officials dictate what he did with his time when his eyes were closed? They had no right to control his mind! They couldn't control his thoughts, so why were they trying? Being locked up in this ghastly prison was bad enough, and having to eat food that smelled like a barnyard was atrocious, but telling a man what he could and could not think spiritually? Prayer was the highest of privileges given by God and should be controlled by no one. Every man, woman, and child on earth had the right to call on their Creator, and no one could take that away from them. Chen wanted to believe this, but the look of contempt on the officer's face told him he would never win that argument.

"We have rules in this prison about what the prisoners can do," the guard said sarcastically, "and practicing your religion is not one of them." He unlocked the gate and stepped into the cell. "I'm going to teach you a lesson about obedience, prisoner, and I hope you will learn from it." He snapped his fingers and another guard hurried forward with a pair of handcuffs.

The guard locked Chen's hands tightly behind him and then gave him a push back toward his mat. "Don't let me catch you praying to your God again," he growled. "Every time you do, I'll come back and pay you a little visit!"

Chen stumbled and almost fell when the officer pushed him but caught his balance. The chain between the cuffs was too short, and that made them very uncomfortable. He tried sitting down on his straw mat, but that was hard too, with his hands cuffed behind him. *This is crazy!* he wanted to shout, and he could feel his resentment and anger growing toward these prison officials. But he knew that would be the dumbest thing he could do right now. For one thing, it was not Christlike. Jesus would never have reacted to mistreatment in that manner.

But other reasons were just as obvious. Chen was a prisoner here. He couldn't control how he was treated in this prison. He couldn't make demands on humanitarian grounds. There were no international inspectors on hand to see that prisoners were treated according to the rules of the Geneva Convention, so why let his anger make him do foolish things?

I must be brave, Chen finally told himself. *Jesus suffered more for me than I could ever suffer for Him. This is the least I can do for my Savior.*

All morning he sat with the handcuffs on, wincing at every move, but try as he might, he could not get comfortable. There seemed to be no good position in which to sit. The cuffs were cruel instruments of torture indeed, and Chen could see they were a very effective form of punishment. The rusty cuffs cut into his wrists, making it hard for him to do anything without experiencing extreme pain.

And the cuffs were taken off for nothing. If a prisoner wanted to eat, he had to get a friend to help him out. Sleeping was very uncomfortable because prisoners could not sleep on their backs and could not turn over easily. Even worse, when a prisoner had to visit the latrine, the cuffs were still there.

What a mess life has become, Chen thought as he lay curled up on the floor in discouragement! *Awful food, mind control, and now these cuffs.* Again he was tempted to feel sorry for himself, and his passages of memorized Scripture were the only thing that kept him going. Verse after well-known verse came to mind, but Psalm 34 seemed to give him courage the most.

"The eyes of the Lord are on the righteous, and His ears are open to their cry. The face of the Lord is against those who do evil. . . . The righteous cry out, and the Lord hears and delivers them out of all their troubles" (Psalm 34:15–17, NKJV). What a blessing these verses were to him as he grappled with the realities of prison life!

He prayed too, now more than ever, keeping in mind that his eyes should be open as the guards demanded. Like Daniel, he knew he needed prayer. The prophet prayed to God three times a day knowing full well the punishment that would be his. *I cannot do less,* Chen told himself, *but I must do it their way. I cannot bow my head. Therefore, I will lift my eyes to heaven. I cannot fold my hands, so I will leave them unfolded. I cannot pray out loud, but I will pray silently.*

That afternoon the prison warden dropped by cell number four. "It's time for honesty and truth!" he announced in a commanding voice, stopping in front of the cell. "I'm taking confessions today as I do every week at this time! Confess to the crimes you have committed against your government, and I will see that you get a lighter sentence!"

Chen sat up painfully. None of the prisoners were responding to the official's sales pitch, and he had to wonder why. Was it all just a charade? What kinds of confessions was he expecting to get from these prisoners? Weren't they in prison for crimes against society like stealing, or rioting, or even murder? Many of the prisoners looked like it. However, from what the officer was saying, it sounded like some of the prisoners had been incarcerated for political reasons.

Maybe their crimes were simply campaigning for shorter work hours at a factory, trying to start a family business, or painting a colorful picture on a storefront. Under the new communist government, such charges were quite common. Maybe there were some who had spoken out against the government, but Chen was guessing many were in on flimsy charges as crazy as the one Chen had been arrested for.

"Do I have any takers?" the warden coaxed. "Come now. I'm not as bad as everyone says I am. I'm not a beast. I'm a humanitarian! You help me, and I'll do my best to help you."

Either the warden was just spouting rhetoric or something else was going on here. Maybe the sessions were more like interrogations than confessions. Maybe the men were being intimidated psychologically or even beaten as part of the confession process. Then again, maybe in this prison it was policy to force confessions from prisoners for the sake of national politics, if nothing else. Maybe the process made the heads of government in their ivory towers feel better about the propaganda they were force feeding the masses on the street every day.

There was no doubt in Chen's mind that the warden would love to interrogate him personally or get a confession out of him, whatever they called it. Fortunately, to Chen's relief, the official did not choose to badger him on this particular day. With handcuffs on and no food in his stomach, he wasn't sure he could have handled it.

The warden stared through the bars at the prisoners, but no one moved or looked at him directly. "What is wrong with you people?" He took hold of the prison bars and began to shake them. "I don't have all day! You are all bad men! You are all criminals! Confess to your crimes, or I will find ways to make you talk!" But still no one took him up on his offer.

77

"I'm done here!" he finally grunted at one of the guards and walked off in a huff.

"Humanitarian!" Chen heard someone smirk under his breath. "So that's what he calls himself!" and from that day forward the nickname stuck. It was clear in the mind of every prisoner that the warden was anything but a humanitarian. He was a bully, but even that was too nice of a title. Regardless of the situation, now whenever anyone saw him coming, a whispered catcall would spread from row to row among the suffering prisoners, "Humanitarian! Humanitarian!"

That night Chen ate his first meal in prison. It was the same corn porridge gruel the prisoners ate at every meal, but it was food, and Chen was finally getting hungry. The gruel was watery and salty with an odor that turned his stomach, but he ate it. Like it or not, he was going to have to get used to it or vomit trying.

After supper, Chen lined up with the others to use the chamber pot, but with over forty men crammed into the cell, there was no place for a walkway. *So this is prison life,* Chen grumbled to himself as he stepped over men and mats on his way to the chamber pot. He felt like a sardine in a can, and there was no privacy. Anyone's business was everybody's business. Then, too, he still had his handcuffs on, and that didn't make the job any easier.

I guess I cannot say I expect better, he sighed. *For Jesus I can afford to be shamed and humiliated. He suffered for me, and I will gladly suffer for Him.*

Later, he sat on his mat as usual and stared at the prison bars. There was nothing else to do. He didn't know how long he sat there, but he guessed it might have been two hours. To pass the time, he recited verses of Scripture that came to mind, and prayed for strength, but by now he knew better than to close his eyes. He was tired but didn't want to lie down too soon. The cuffs were still on, cutting into his wrists, and his back ached from having his hands bound in such an uncomfortable position. The floor was hard and cold, and with the cuffs on, it was going to be a long night.

Thank You, Lord, Chen kept repeating to himself, and he tried to mean it. *This was my first full day of class in the Lord's school of prison. I have learned much, and for that I am grateful.*

Chapter 19

The morning of Chen's third day in prison dawned, and with it the realization that his new life was here to stay. How long would he be in this place? He didn't know. One month? Two months? Six? Was it possible he might be here for years? He didn't want to think of that prospect, but with the new communist government under Mao Zedong's control, who could say?

As Chen sat on his mat feeling sorry for himself and thinking about what lay ahead, he remembered a comment made by one of his friends years before. "If Jesus is with you, even prison can become a paradise." Chen knew this was good advice, and for now he drew comfort just knowing that Jesus was with him here in the prison cell.

Please Lord, he prayed, *help me accept this burden You ask me to bear. I pray that I can be a witness for You, especially under these conditions.*

At breakfast, the men all lined up again, and again they ate their regular ration of corn gruel. Chen could not carry the cup of porridge because his hands were still cuffed behind his back. Nor could he feed himself the porridge with a spoon, so Huang Fu offered to feed him.

It was an extremely humbling experience, and the prison officials knew it. It was bad enough that Chen had to eat food that smelled this awful, but having to have someone spoon-feed him made him feel like a baby.

Still, before eating his breakfast, Chen paused to thank God for the meal. Out of habit, he bowed his head and folded his cuffed hands behind him in prayer. The guard who had cuffed him happened to be passing the cell at that moment and could not believe his eyes.

"What on earth are you doing?" he asked incredulously with his hands on his hips.

Chen was caught by surprise. Too late he realized his mistake, but he didn't miss a beat. "I'm praying," he replied with dignity. "I'm thanking God for my food."

The guard could only shake his head. "You don't get it, do you?" he stammered. "When you show stupidity like this, we can hardly give you mercy! The government has decreed that praying is illegal, even in prison! That's why your hands are cuffed right now!"

"Yes, sir. I know, sir," was all Chen could say. He could see how ridiculous the whole thing must look. Why would anyone submit himself to such humiliating treatment? To anyone looking on, it didn't make sense.

But to Chen, it made perfect sense! Come what may, he was going to pray to his Maker. Every day he was going to pray to God! He would never stop praying no matter what they did to him! In hard times, he needed more prayer, not less! They could punish him, and he was still going to pray! They could whip him, beat him, and even kill him, but in any and all circumstances, he was going to pray to his Father and bring honor and glory to His name.

The guard stood staring at Chen a few moments longer, then shook his head and turned away. "I don't believe it!" he mumbled in total disbelief.

By now, of course, everyone knew Chen was a Christian, and that was exactly what Chen wanted. His greatest desire was to be faithful to God and witness for the precious truths of the Bible.

After supper that night, the guard came into Chen's cell and took his handcuffs off. "I'm removing them," he said, "but don't forget I have the power to put them on again. And don't forget why they were put on in the first place."

The days crawled by slowly, and Chen wondered what it would be like for his little flock of church members on his first Sabbath away from them. Would their faith in God be strong in spite of his capture? Would they take the risk of meeting together? He knew they would pray for him, and he prayed fervently for them in turn.

He wasn't worried for himself because he now realized that Sabbath observance in this place was probably not going to be much of a trial. How could it be? He wasn't allowed to do anything. There were no work requirements. No mandatory duties. There was nothing he could do in this prison that would cause him to violate the seventh-day Sabbath commandment.

But that didn't mean it would be easy. In this place, he would be deprived of all the usual things he loved to do so much on the Sabbath. He wouldn't be able to read his Bible. He wasn't allowed to have one. He couldn't pray publicly in the prison, and he couldn't leave to worship with his church members in Wu Xi.

But then again, there were the little things he could do in worship, and it was these things that would draw him near to heaven's door. He could pray silently, if nothing else. He could recite his Bible verses. Now and then he could even pull out the hidden scrap of paper and read the verses he had written on it when he first arrived.

As he imagined, that first Sabbath was a real blessing for him. The prayers, Bible verses, and quiet time in communion with his heavenly Father were a real joy and comfort to him. He would have liked to share the experience with his fellow prisoners and explain the biblical truths about the Sabbath rest day. But that was impossible at the moment, a difficult thing to do since he wasn't allowed to talk with any of them about his faith. That part would have to come later. For now, he would simply be the man God wanted him to be, rest in the Father's care, and truly claim the promises given him as a child of the King.

On the eve of September 30, there was great excitement among the prisoners because the next day would be a Chinese national day. What the warden would give them for a feast in celebration was all they could think about, and the men were making simple bets on what they expected to get. Would it be wonton soup made with pork and cabbage, duck and dumplings, or fish with rice?

As bedtime approached, the prisoners were giddy in anticipation, and their eyes brightened as they talked about the good things they would eat the next day. It was as if nothing could get them down. Chen thought it was amazing that the promise of something special could change the tone of everyone's attitude in this distressing place. It was like magic.

But the next morning at breakfast, they were all disappointed when they were greeted by the same watery gruel. Their hopes had been so high, and Chen realized now that the promise of something special had been just a rumor started by the prisoners among themselves. What a tragedy for them all! Simple though the thought of good food might have been, the real truth was the worst form of torture yet.

Around lunchtime, the prisoners could smell meat cooking, but again they were left frustrated by disappointment. The meat was being prepared for the prison guards and officers only. At supper, however, they were finally given some fish, a great treat to supplement their regular diet. The fish was tough and salty, but to Chen it was like food from a king's table.

And yet many of the prisoners complained that they had not been given a meal fit for celebration. Like Israel wandering in the desert, they did not recognize the value of the simple blessings granted them by their heavenly Father. If the prisoners could have known the hard times that were coming in the next few months, they would have been so grateful for the little they had received. They would have considered the fish a fine delicacy compared to the starvation rations to come. All complaining would have disappeared, gone like the warm winds of autumn on that October afternoon.

The next evening, the warden came down again to the main floor of the prison. "I am your best friend in here," he announced loudly so that everyone could hear. "I am your humanitarian, and don't you forget it! I am not a beast but am actually quite accommodating to your needs as you will see." He cleared his throat importantly.

"Tonight I have a surprise for you. We are going to let you write a letter to one of your relatives. You can greet them and tell them how you are doing, but do not speak about this prison. And do not talk about your religious beliefs. All letters will be censored before sending them out, of course, so be positive." He glanced around the crowded cell, "If you need anything like a towel or soap or toothbrush, now is the time to make your requests to your friends and families in the letter."

Chen was relieved to hear such news. It would be nice to be able to wash his hands before he ate, and he hadn't brushed his teeth since the morning he left the mountain. However, he doubted the prison officers were as thoughtful as they were making themselves out to be by giving the prisoners a chance to write letters. No doubt this was another means of propaganda to make everyone feel the conditions at this prison weren't so bad.

However, it was true that Chen had no personal belongings with him at the prison, and this was his one chance to get some. There was only one way to see that happen. He must write a letter.

But who could he write to? He had no idea where his father and mother might be in their travels for evangelism. He could write to his church members who lived right here in Wu Xi. It might be that they had no idea where he was, though it had been clear to everyone in town the day he was arrested that he was likely to be jailed. He and the MPs had left in quite a hurry.

Chen wrote the letter taking great pains to be sure it was free from any comments about the prison conditions. He didn't want to lie and tell his members that he was being treated well, but neither did he want to say things that would keep the letter from reaching its destination. "How is everyone? I miss you all," he wrote cheerfully enough. "If you could send me soap and a towel, I would much appreciate it. Also send a toothbrush and two shirts, and some long underwear for cold weather would be nice."

He would have liked to include a choice verse of Scripture in the letter to encourage the little flock, but, of course, that was forbidden. Nothing about his faith in God could be included; this meant he couldn't write about his belief that God had brought him to this prison for a reason, which he was sure would have helped the church members greatly. Some would know by the tone of his letter that he was being unusually cheerful. They would surely read between the lines for the hidden truth about exactly how he was faring.

And then as he waited, he began to count the days for a reply by mail.

Chains in China

He kept track of the days by making marks with a pencil on the floor under his mat. The days dragged by slowly and painfully, but the whole process was more hopeful somehow knowing there was a reality outside these prison walls, a whole different world out there. Chen might be locked up inside this dungeon of doom, but outside, people were walking to and fro in the streets, free to come and go as they pleased. People were living normal lives of happiness and plenty, and they could get the things to him that he so desperately needed. There were people out there who loved him. There were people out there who cared. There were people out there praying for him.

Chapter 20

The days came and went like the pages of a book. Chen worked his way up to spot number twenty in the prisoners' line-up of straw mats lying on the jail cell floor. Prisoners left and others arrived to take their place. Every time one of them was released, Chen was bumped forward one place in the lineup, which meant he was that much farther away from the foul latrine. This was considered a real accomplishment, as accomplishments went in the life of inmates at the Wu Xi prison.

However, other than this, there was nothing to break the monotony of prison life, and Chen was afraid he was going to go crazy with the sameness of it all. He couldn't read—he had no books. He couldn't witness to the other men or give them Bible studies, much as they needed it—the prisoners weren't allowed to talk to one another. He couldn't even watch the clouds go by because there were no windows in the prison.

One evening after supper, however, there came a real break in the numbing effect prison life was having on Chen. A guard opened the gate and told Chen to follow him. What did he want? Chen wondered. Was the guard releasing him to be sent home? Not a chance in a thousand! That would be too easy. Chen had prayed countless times that God would deliver him from this awful prison, but his heart told him God's work for him here was not yet complete.

Was he in trouble again for something he had done in the jail cell? He hadn't been talking, just a little whispering sometimes, maybe, but only when it was absolutely necessary. No, this was probably something more serious. Chen had seen many of his fellow prisoners come back to the cell after long periods of time away with the officers. Some of them looked like they had suffered mental anguish. Some looked as if they had been beaten. Some looked worse.

Chen didn't want to think about where the guard was taking him or what he might do to him, but he realized he needed to brace himself for any possibility. Chinese communist officers were said to be capable of anything. In the few seconds it took them to walk the distance of the corridor, his mind thought of a thousand things.

Would the officers interrogate him and ask him questions about his church group? The names of his members, maybe? Surely they knew all the names in the group he had worshiped with anyway, though Chen was determined he was going to give them nothing they didn't already have in the way of identifications.

Would the officers torture him, maybe, using bright lights, water, bamboo, or sharp things as he had heard so much about in prisons like this? They couldn't threaten him with starvation, of that he was sure. He was already receiving such bad food—and so little of it—they would surely know that tactic would be ineffective to get information out of him.

Or worse, would they try to get him to give up his faith in God? Of all Chen's fears, this was the worst. They could do anything and everything to him, but his faith in God was the most precious of all his possessions—if one could call it that. He had very little else to help him keep his dignity here in this prison. Daily, he was forced to live in filth. He had no water to wash himself to stay clean. He had no change of clothes. There was no space for him to exercise properly, and he couldn't shave. Exercise and a shave alone would have done wonders for his self-esteem and morale.

There was no doubt in Chen's mind that prayer and faith in God were keeping him going, and he could not afford to lose either one. Everything else he wanted or desired or so desperately needed in this prison paled in importance next to his dependence on God. He would not give up his faith! He would not relinquish his hold on the promises of God's Word! No matter what they did to him, by God's grace and strength he would stand tall like an oak tree planted by the river of God. A verse of Scripture came to mind suddenly, and Chen clung to the strength it gave him. *"Be strong and of good courage; do not be afraid, nor be dismayed, for the Lord your God is with you wherever you go"* (Joshua 1:9, NKJV).

When he and the guard had walked a simple maze of corridors, they came to a formidable-looking steel door. Chen guessed it must be an interrogation room, and his heart skipped a beat despite his resolutions about how strong he must be for God.

As they entered the room, Chen saw two officers about his age sitting in chairs behind a table. One of them was clearly a man who had been trained in the military, and his face was severely pockmarked. His shock of hair was a steely gray like his eyes, and a cold sneer curled his lip even when he wasn't talking. Chen had seen him before and knew his name was Hong.

The other officer was much taller, and his clothes hung on him like a scarecrow's. He had big hands and even bigger ears, it seemed, and his hair was buzzed shorter than the fuzz on a peach.

"Have a seat," Hong said coldly, pointing to a chair at one end of the room.

Chen sat down cautiously. Things did not look good. The stage was set for an ugly session with the prison officials just as he had suspected. To this point, other than bad food and handcuffs, Chen had suffered little at the hand of prison officers. But it appeared this would all change now. There was no doubt in his mind that these officers intended to treat him badly. Actually, he was surprised they had waited so long.

His eye swept the room in a glance. There was a light in the corner, though it wasn't a bright one, and it didn't look like the officers intended to grill him with it shining in his eyes as interrogators often did. Chen didn't see any sharp instruments of torture nearby, nor the tubs full of water that he had imagined might be in a room for such interrogations.

Maybe that would come later. Chen prayed that God would spare him unnecessary pain, and that the angels would be near. Without thinking, he bowed his head, forgetting the officers were watching him. *Please Lord,* he prayed, *don't let me fail You in this moment for lack of courage. Keep me faithful to Your name and Your cause. The battle is not mine but Yours. You won it long ago at Calvary. Give me the right things to say, Lord. You are my only hope.*

It was a simple prayer born of simple faith. Chen raised his head to look at the officers, and almost instantly the words of Matthew 10 flashed into his mind. *"When they deliver you up, do not worry about how or what you should speak. For it will be given to you in that hour what you should speak; for it is not you who speak, but the Spirit of your Father who speaks in you"* (Matthew 10:19, 20, NKJV).

He half-glanced around the room again, as though someone there had prompted him with such a thought. And then he knew. It was the Holy Spirit, just as the verse of Scripture had promised. God was here in this room with Chen. The angels were here with him to make him brave. They would give him the right words to say, and the strength to do it.

Hong stood up and walked to where Chen was sitting. "You are praying to your God?" he lifted his hands scornfully in the air. "Who is this God?" He shrugged as if in answer to his own question and began walking around Chen's chair. "He cannot come to your rescue here! He will not help you escape from us!"

Chen bowed his head again. It seemed the right thing to do out of respect for the officers.

"Tell us about the twenty-sixth of September," Hong said sternly. "What were you doing in town that day?"

Chen glanced up again. He stared forward, but did not look at either officer. "Sir, I was asked to perform a wedding."

"Who gave you permission to conduct the wedding in the village?" came the questioner's machine-gun reply.

"The couple to be married already had permission from the government. They are Christians, and there were no other Christian ministers left in town, so they wanted me to conduct the wedding vows."

"You know churches are not allowed to perform such ceremonies," Hong kept on.

"That is true," Chen admitted. "We used to do such things in the church before the churches were all shut down. Now we are not allowed to have a church building, so we were conducting the wedding at the groom's house."

"The couple could have found someone to do it for them legally!" Hong was clearly not interested in Chen's explanations.

"They tried but could find no one. Everyone was too afraid to conduct the ceremony, so I performed the wedding," Chen admitted, "but only because there was no one else to do it. The people were happy to have me do it, and I never took a coin in pay—"

"We are not concerned about the happiness of the people when they break the law!" Hong interrupted. "Their sincerity and yours are of no interest to us!"

Chapter 21

id you pray at the wedding?" Hong added, changing gears in the conversation.

Chen hesitated only a moment. "Yes, sir, we did. It is customary to offer prayers at Christian weddings. It is considered a sure way to send the young couple on their way with blessings and best wishes."

"So this is considered a form of good luck?'

"Christians do not believe in good luck, sir. We would say these blessings are from heaven," Chen added. "It is the God of heaven who gives all such blessings."

"I do not want to hear about your God!" Hong snapped, his voice filled with hate. "Religion is forbidden by the great Mao Zedong!"

Chen remained silent.

"What about the families you met with in Wu Xi?" Hong jabbed. "We know all about your activities with them, how you met with people to preach. Who gave you permission to conduct family worships in town? Were they religious meetings?"

"Yes," Chen replied confidently. "We did not think it wise to hide the fact that we were involved in religious meetings. We are Christians. In the Bible, God has asked His people to meet together every Sabbath to worship, and that is what we were doing. We are not ashamed of it." Chen knew he had to be honest, but he was worried for the welfare of his church members. His only concern was that none of them be punished and suffer like him in prison.

Hong glared at Chen. "The government does not allow for such meetings, and yet you met illegally! You are not allowed to meet and proselytize people! You cannot have meetings public or private to convert people to your religious organization! It is forbidden under the laws of the new revolution! What is the full name of your organization?" His angry questions were relentless now, like a barrage of machine-gun fire.

"The Seventh-day Adventist Church," Chen replied, realizing Hong was not getting what he had come for in this interrogation. What the officer really wanted was a confession of wrongdoing. He wanted a tearful admission that would dig Chen in even deeper than he already was.

"You cannot say you are part of a Seventh-day Adventist Church!" Hong barked. "If you want to meet, you must do so under the Three-Self Organization. You are aware of this program." It was more of a statement than a question.

"The government department of religions says that all people who wish to be part of a religious organization must enlist under the 'Three-Self' clause," Chen replied dutifully. "Christians included."

"That is correct," Hong half smiled, his voice dripping with sarcasm as if he might be getting somewhere. "Christians can have a religious experience individually but not as a group. In your case, not as a church," he stabbed his finger at Chen. "And that means they cannot be paid to work for that organization either. They cannot receive a salary from any church or religious group."

He stared at Chen. "If you are against the principles of Three-Self, then you are against the government, and that means you are against the revolution of Master Mao Zedong." He said the words as though they were holy, as though Mao Zedong was himself an ambassador sent from heaven. "What do you have to say to these charges?" growled Hong. "Is it not true that you are guilty of them all?"

Chen knew everything Hong had said was true. Under Mao Zedong's new regime, anyone of any faith was not allowed to evangelize, whether Christian or Muslim or Buddhist. And receiving a regular salary for such services in these churches, as Chen had been doing for the last few months, was forbidden. Hong was right about all this, but that didn't mean Chen was doing wrong in God's eyes. Earthly rulers came and went, but God and His Word would always be around.

The Bible verse about obeying God rather than men came to mind (Acts 5:29), but Chen didn't use it on his interrogators. It didn't seem to be the right time to take such a stand—at least not yet. He was sure Hong wouldn't understand. He would just think Chen was defying him and trying to be rude.

But Chen believed every word of that verse and was willing to risk his freedom for it. He knew the key to his future lay in that statement, and he knew that his unwillingness to stop preaching the gospel would keep him in prison for a very long time. On the other hand, if he would confess that he was guilty of all the "crimes" he was being accused of, and promise not to preach again, they would probably let him go home.

But, of course, Chen knew he would never do that. Like Joseph, Daniel, and the three Hebrews in the fiery furnace, he must stand up for the right no matter what any government might say. Like Jesus' disciples, he must be willing to tell the gospel story regardless of the consequences. No matter what bad things Satan and his allies did to God's people down through the ages, like his forefathers, Chen must obey God rather than men even if the enemies of God didn't understand.

"We have heard other things too," Hong was saying.

Chen blinked hard to bring himself back to reality. He needed to stay focused. He needed to stay with the interrogators in their questioning.

"We have heard strange tales about what you do at your meetings with the church folks," the officer added. "It is reported that you sometimes heal people of their diseases." He stared at Chen. His voice was harsh and unfeeling, but his eyes told a different story, as if he might truly be interested in such things.

"It is said that when you preach you have power to cast out evil spirits," Hong sounded skeptical. "We do not believe in demons," he added, although Chen wondered if there might be something in Hong's background to convince him otherwise.

Chen took a deep breath. "I don't cast out the evil spirits," he explained. "Only God can do that. I merely speak for Him."

"So you admit to having cast out demons?"

"God casts out the demons."

"We don't believe in demons, and we don't believe in God."

"Then how do you explain the supernatural behavior of the demon-possessed? These people can tell you what you did in the secret chambers of your house. They are incredibly strong and can lift things a hundred times their own weight." Chen was on a roll, and it seemed he was saying all the right things. "And how do you explain the fact that I have cast out such demons?" Chen added more softly. "If there is no such thing as people with incredible supernatural powers far beyond the range of human possibility, then why try to convince me they don't exist? Why claim there are no evil forces at work and there is no God in heaven who has power over them all? I only speak for God and help deliver these poor folks from the power of the evil one who would destroy their souls."

Hong and the other officer stared at Chen, neither one saying anything for a few moments, and then Hong finally found his voice. "That will be all for now," he said rather brusquely, as if he were in a hurry to be rid of Chen. "Read this affidavit of interrogation and sign it, indicating that you were here and have been questioned by us." He pushed a paper and pen toward Chen on the table between them. "After that you may go."

Chen did as he was told and was then escorted back to his cell. It had been a grueling hour in the interrogation chamber, and he was glad it was over. As he settled in for the night, he thought about everything he had been through in the few weeks since coming to this prison. He had experienced it all: bad food, cramped quarters, rusty handcuffs, the silent treatment, an open latrine just centimeters away from where he slept, and now an interrogation that had turned out much better than he could have hoped for.

God is good, Chen told himself as he lay on his straw mat staring up at the dark ceiling. *I cannot complain. I have always asked that God let me serve Him where I am needed most, and right now, I guess I am needed here most.*

He closed his eyes as if to shut out the night sounds echoing through the prison. Prisoners around him snored, some of them almost raucously. Guards above him paced their routine pathways on the metal catwalk. And somewhere a night owl was calling to him in this death trap of a prison.

Chen was uncomfortable from lying on the hard floor. He was in pain from the raw cuts made by handcuffs on his wrists and the growling of his empty stomach. But this was where God wanted him to be, and that was comfort enough for Chen right now.

"Wait on the Lord!" Chen breathed his final prayer for the night. *"Be of good courage, and He shall strengthen your heart. Wait, I say, on the Lord!"* (Psalm 27:14, NKJV).

Chapter 22

One morning without warning, the warden suddenly appeared outside the cell door. "This is a shakedown!" he shouted. "Everybody on your feet! Guards, open the gate!"

He strutted into the jail cell as if he were the most important person in the world, and by the way the prisoners jumped to attention, one would have thought he was.

"Prisoners, we will be examining your personal belongings this morning. Step away from your sleeping mat and wait until we complete the search. We will also be doing body checks. If there is any contraband, you will be punished." The warden's face seemed chiseled in stone, but Chen could tell this would be the highlight of his day. And maybe it was. Who wouldn't want a little bit of excitement around here to break the monotony of prison life?

Chen jumped to attention with the others. Cooperation was the name of the game here, and he didn't want to give the warden any chance to zero in on him. And what would he find anyway? Chen had nothing to hide, did he? What he didn't know was that the warden had called for the surprise shakedown for the purpose of finding something he could use against Chen specifically. If he could do that, he would have Chen right where he wanted him. And he needed that since Chen had gained the upper hand that night in the interrogation chamber.

The shakedown began with the guards searching every inch of the jail cell. They rummaged through everyone's things—their blankets, their personal belongings, and underneath their sleeping mats. However, it soon became evident that the warden was spending much of his time and energy on Chen's area. Then he turned his focus on Chen himself, searching him from head to toe. He looked in his shoes and in his hair, and he even made him take his clothes off so he could search through them. Fortunately for Chen, the warden found nothing and finally left in disgust. He had been so sure he would find something with which to condemn Chen, but he had failed.

An hour later, however, he came back in a hurry as if he had received an inside tip about where to look. Without hesitation, he and a guard came marching back into the cell and ordered Chen to get up. The warden went straight to Chen's pillow, and to Chen's dismay, there inside the lining they found the piece of paper with the Bible verses on it.

The inscriptions were written in Chinese characters so tiny they could hardly be read, but to the warden that was unimportant. He was so happy he nearly danced out of the cell with the piece of paper clutched tightly in his hand. "We've got it! We've got it!" he shouted, as if he had made some great discovery. He clanged the cell gate behind him and turned to gloat at Chen. "This is the contraband we've been looking for, and it will be used as evidence against you, criminal!" He waved the little paper at Chen. "We were right about you! Even in prison you are an enemy of the revolution, and I intend to make you pay for it!"

Chen could not believe his eyes and ears. "Who have I harmed?" he called after the warden. "It was just a few Bible verses! How can such a thing be forbidden? I sit here with nothing to do all day, so I write verses that I remember."

But the warden was not listening and rushed off to plot his next move against Chen. The whole thing was a sham! Chen could only shake his head at the foolish charade engineered by the warden. Was this truly the height of glory for the warden and his officers? Was this kind of triumph all that he and his accomplices had to live for?

As Chen had suspected, one of the prisoners had reported the hidden paper hoping to gain special favor with the warden. The thought of such a thing made Chen's blood boil. He didn't even want to think about who the turncoat might be, but whoever it was, he had to be sneaky. He must have been watching Chen closely to see him put the piece of paper away. Chen hadn't brought the little scrap of paper out of its hiding place more than half a dozen times since he had hidden it.

It was hard to say what would happen next.

The question was, What should he expect now in the wake of the warden's discovery? The prison official seemed quite jubilant about the whole thing as though he expected a promotion from his superiors for his detective work. But really now, Chen wondered, how much misfortune could a little piece of paper like that bring a prisoner? He was already sleeping on the filthy floor, undergoing interrogations, eating porridge that tasted like a barnyard, and getting handcuffed when he whispered to other prisoners. Were things going to get even worse? It was possible.

There was no doubt in Chen's mind that he would be punished for his "crime." It was clear there would be some sort of penalty, that he would be made to pay the price of disobedience, but what that might be was his only concern.

Chains in China

God would be with him to help him through the ordeal, of that he was sure.

However, when the warden came back at noon to give his verdict, Chen was hardly prepared for the sentence passed down on him, and he had difficulty disguising his surprise.

"For your insolence you will miss the noon meal today," the warden addressed Chen harshly as though he were a child. "Furthermore, at supper tonight you will make a confession to the other prisoners. You will apologize for your disrespect of Chairman Mao and his honorable principles which you have violated." The warden glanced over at the full poster picture of Mao Zedong on the corridor wall of the prison.

"You will also express your regret for violating our prison code," he added, "and for causing a disruption to the lives of these men by bringing contraband into this place. Now think about what you have done and be ashamed!"

Chen watched the warden depart down the corridor and tried to stifle a smile. Did the warden really think Chen would miss the smelly porridge? Even now, these many weeks since his arrival, he still had not fallen in love with mealtime. And did the warden think a confession was going to change anything in Chen's mind? Did he think an apology of that sort would be humiliating?

Still, what the warden was asking would be no simple thing. Any kind of political confession to Chairman Mao could be a compromise for a Christian. It required that Chen salute the revolutionary, and for a Seventh-day Adventist that was a problem.

Even worse, it implied that Chen was willing to recant his belief in the God of heaven. Like the worshiping of Nebuchadnezzar's golden image on the Plains of Dura, such an act would in fact express allegiance to a godless leader of a government that claimed there was no God.

And Chen's spiritual instincts were correct. Mao Zedong was not a leader any self-respecting Christian would want to honor. He could not know it, but this revolutionary ruler would go on to become one of the worst despots in history! In the decade to come, Mao Zedong would kill tens of millions in concentration camps through starvation and genocide.

All that afternoon Chen thought about the apology he would have to give that evening. He knew his confession would require great humbleness and tact. However, it would also be an excellent time for him to witness for his faith. It would be a prime opportunity to tell everyone why he was in this prison and what he stood for. Jesus had died for the men in the Wu Xi prison, and they needed to know it.

The afternoon hours dragged by, and Chen spent the time in prayer. There was little need to worry about what he would and wouldn't say in his testimony.

He would leave those details up to God. After all, that was God's specialty—speaking to the heart when a man needed it most. *"A word fitly spoken is like apples of gold in settings of silver,"* thought Chen (Proverbs 25:11, NKJV). God would give him the words he needed to say. They would be like streams of living water to the heart of each prisoner.

After supper that night, Chen stood up to confess his "mistake," and the warden was there to hear it, hanging on to every word as if they were music to his ears. To speak in front of the other prisoners did not frighten Chen. It was the injustice of it all that bothered him the most. To put it bluntly, having to give a confession for something as trivial as a scrap of paper with Bible verses written on it seemed childish indeed. And having to give such a confession in this loathsome prison where prisoners wore nothing but rags for clothing made it seem even more ridiculous.

Chen took a deep breath. *Help me, Lord,* he prayed. *I need wisdom.* He knew his confession needed to be more than just a statement of wrong. It needed to have a built-in testimony for Jesus. He had given testimonies in church countless times before, but this was his first time giving one in prison.

"Most of you know by now why I am in this prison," Chen began. "I'm a Seventh-day Adventist preacher, incarcerated here because I met regularly with fellow believers to worship the Lord God of heaven and earth. I preached from the Bible daily. Interestingly enough, the written words of the Bible have been used against me because I dared to write them on a small scrap of paper in this prison cell. And yet it is these words that give me hope and a reason to live each day. These words make me a better citizen and a better man. They tell me of Jesus who came to die for my sins and save me from the pain and sadness of this world."

Chen hurried on, afraid he would lose his nerve and the courage to say what needed to be said. "I have come to make a confession of guilt tonight," he continued. "I must confess that I am guilty of being a sinner before God, but Jesus died to save me, to make me clean inside for all the things I've done wrong. *'If we confess our sins, He is faithful and just to forgive us our sins and to cleanse us from all unrighteousness.'* *'For God so loved the world that He gave His only begotten Son, that whoever believes in Him should not perish but have everlasting life'* [1 John 1:9, NKJV; John 3:16, NKJV].

"For this reason I love the Lord, and for this reason I must give my allegiance to Him." Chen's face was serious. "I do not want to dishonor Chairman Mao and his new regime, but I cannot bring dishonor on my God either. There can be no conflict between my country and my God, and where such a conflict should arise, I must obey God rather than men."

Chains in China

Silence filled the prison cell as every prisoner listened intently. No one said a word or moved. It was as if each man were at the judgment bar of heaven hearing the voice of God for the first time. But the effect went even further. The inmates from other cell blocks in the prison could be seen stretching their necks out to hear what this preacher man was saying in cell number four. Even the warden seemed mesmerized by Chen's confession of faith. But the moment was short lived.

Chapter 23

"top!" the warden suddenly sputtered, his face a picture of confusion and anger. "What is this you are saying? I have asked that you make a confession of guilt, but here you are now talking of this Jesus! What do you mean by this nonsense?" It was clear the warden had been moved by Chen's Christian testimony but then maybe caught himself, realizing how it must look for a government official to be moved by the words of a prisoner.

"I cannot allow this!" the warden growled, back to his old self again. "You have shamed yourself and your fellow inmates by this confession! For this you will be punished yet again. Where is your spot on the prison floor?" he glanced here and there in search of Chen's rolled up sleeping mat.

"I am now at spot number twenty," Chen pointed to his place along the wall near the middle of the sleeping mats.

"I see," the warden said slowly. "You have worked hard to get to this place in the line, have you not?" And then his face took on a look of meanness and spite. "I think you have lessons to learn yet in this prison, foolish one. From spot number twenty, you will go back to your original spot at the end of the line." He glanced toward the latrine and gave Chen one of his evil smiles. "You will like that better, will you not, preacher man? It will feel more like home."

There was nothing for Chen to say. Not for a minute did he want to move back near the chamber pot and open latrine, but neither did he want to bow to the whims of a petty warden! And the punishment would do nothing to change Chen's mind about his faith in God. To give such a confession as a prisoner and then be punished for it might be humiliating to some, but for Chen it was an honor. For a moment, he had tasted what all God's people feel at one time or another in their pilgrim journey. He had testified of the Father's love in sending His only Son. He had reminded his fellow prisoners that they, too, needed a Savior to wash away their sins. He had sensed the whisper of angels' wings bowing low to see him stand for the right.

Unfortunately, it was all wasted on the warden. If the man hadn't been so busy chastising Chen, he might have had time to hear the angels' wings himself.

Chen had given the testimony of his life, and everyone in the prison had heard it—even the warden. He had appeared shell-shocked and a bit tongue-tied by this preacher's simple faith. When he had finally realized the effect Chen's witness was having in the prison, he had stopped him, but it was too late. The seeds of the gospel had been planted. The other prisoners had listened to Chen's words and been touched by them. They knew Chen was a Christian and now understood the expression of peace they saw every day on his face. The warden had meant to punish Chen for writing the Scripture verses, but he ended up rewarding him instead by giving him a chance to share his testimony for Jesus. It was the defining moment of Chen's days in prison thus far.

Weeks passed and everything returned to normal once again. Life in the Wu Xi prison was tedious and boring at best, but one thing was sure: it held few surprises. One always knew what to expect.

One day, Chen was again called to the interrogation chamber. He could tell the officer assigned to question him was from his own home province because his accent betrayed him. The official seemed like a kind man, though Chen tried to remember that this officer, like any other, was an interrogator and therefore obliged to get information out of him. It was not a nice job. From what Chen had seen, the business of interrogation could turn nice guys into ogres.

"Sit down, young man," the interrogator looked up when Chen walked into the room. He was going through Chen's folder on the table and seemed very interested in what he found there.

"I see that you are from the working class," he said cheerfully. "You have a good worker's record, and that speaks well for you." He laid down the folder and smiled at Chen. "I think we share many of the same experiences. You see, I also am of the working class. My name is Quan," he bowed his head slightly. "For years, I was a pipe fitter in a chemical plant.

"We laborers have to stick together if we want respect," he continued. "We have all been exploited and oppressed at some time in our lives, but communism's working class rules the country now. Being a laborer is an honor and a great source of pride for all of us. Laborers can build a better world and a better economy—

"Would you like some tea?" Quan asked, interrupting himself to reach for a teapot at the end of the table.

Chen nodded. "Thank you. That would be nice." He liked this officer. They seemed to have so much in common. He felt as if he had finally found a friend, someone who might be an advocate for him here in this prison. But could he really trust the interrogator? That remained to be seen.

Chains in China

"You are an intelligent man, Chen," the officer said, taking a sip of tea from his cup. "Tell me, why are you so superstitious about the religion of Christianity? There is so much of your religion that does not make sense. For instance, why do you worship your God on Saturdays? And why do you speak so highly of Ellen White, this woman from America? Her books are not good. We consider them as one of the poisons from the West."

Chen said nothing as Quan studied him carefully. Would this be a game of cat and mouse, a standoff in which both he and the interrogator hoped to gain the edge?

"You may speak," the interrogator finally said, leaning back in his chair. "I would like to know what you are thinking."

"I think that you do not understand Christianity," Chen suggested. "Have you not known good Christian people, missionaries, perhaps, who have given their lives for people they don't know in a strange land they cannot call their own? Have you not met those who have sacrificed their lives for their faith? The God I serve asks that His followers be willing to give up everything to tell the good news of salvation. And what is this good news? Jesus came to die for a lost world that knew Him not—plain and simple. That is what Christianity is all about."

"You are speaking gibberish!" the interrogator snapped. "It is all foolishness and will get you nowhere! You are too young to be throwing your life away on such nonsense! Listen to the great Chairman Mao instead. Follow his lead and you will live long and prosper!" He shook his head as though he pitied Chen. "You must think seriously about your future."

Chen nodded again. "Thank you for your concern, sir. I really do cherish my future. To be an honest laborer is a good thing if it brings with it an honorable career. As to the communistic ideas of Chairman Mao? They may be a good thing for our country, but I also care deeply about my religion. I don't want to go against my beliefs."

The interrogator's face flushed with anger. "You are into the poison so deep, I'm afraid you will never get out! I came here to help you, young man! I felt sure I could convince you to give up your silly notions like the one about honoring your Christian Sabbath!" His eyes narrowed. "Is that not the reason you lost your old job at the pharmaceutical factory in Shanghai?"

There was silence in the interrogation chamber as Chen bowed his head respectfully. "It is true I lost my job in Shanghai because I chose to honor God's Sabbath. But I do not regret it to this day. I cannot give up my Sabbaths. They mean too much to me, but I thank you, honorable Quan. I will not forget your kindness to me."

The interrogator slapped the table with his hand and stood to his feet. "If you do not want my help, there's nothing more I can do for you here! However, I feel I must tell you that from this day forward, things will not go well for you here at the Wu Xi prison. The greatest achievement for the warden and his officers is to persuade each prisoner to give a confession of loyalty to the policies of Chairman Mao. If you are stubborn and do not give the confession, the warden will become tough as nails! He will never let you out of here!"

Chen's mouth dropped open at this announcement. *Not let me go!* Chen almost gasped. Had he heard right? The idea of never leaving this prison was utterly depressing, and it terrified Chen, making him want to panic. He had tried to help Quan understand the reasons why being a Christian was so important, but he knew now that he had failed miserably. Had he said all the wrong things, or was the interrogator so far from God that he could not see truth even if it was staring him full in the face?

Chen walked back to the jail cell feeling more dejected now than he had at any time since he first came to the prison. He was hungry, tired, and emotionally drained after interrogation round number two. And he was homesick. More than anything, he wanted to go home to his church family in Wu Xi. Unfortunately, it didn't look as if that was going to happen any time soon. Not if the warden had anything to say about it.

An overwhelming desire to be free washed over Chen now as he thought about what the interrogator had said. If he did not give up his notions of God, the Bible, and the Sabbath, the warden would never let him out of here!

By now winter had set in. With the arrival of December came colder weather, and with the cold came incredible attacks of shivering. Chen's clothes were becoming worn and threadbare in places. Some days he shivered so much he thought his teeth would chatter right out of his mouth! He developed a cough too, and that should have worried him a little. Actually, it should have worried him a lot.

Fortunately, he had finally received the long-legged underwear he'd asked for in the letters he wrote to his Wu Xi church members. The underwear was made of cotton and kept him much warmer. He had also woven a new thicker mat of straw so he wouldn't have to sleep on the old prison mat that was now thin and worn.

However, even with the underwear and new mat, Chen was still colder than cold! The prison food could never provide enough nourishment for him. Even worse, food was becoming scarcer in China because a famine had hit the country. Everyone was feeling that in the prison diet now. The porridge was thinner than ever with even fewer vegetables floating in its watery gruel.

But one highlight seemed to hover on the horizon of their happiness. Everyone was looking forward to the approaching Chinese New Year, when they hoped they would be given a special meal. There was nothing more exciting than a good meal on a happy holiday, and Chinese New Year was the biggest and best holiday of the year!

However, as the holiday approached, Chen wondered if he would even be able to eat this meal. Meat was sure to be on the menu, and that meant the prisoners would likely be given pork. Pork was without a doubt the favorite meat of every man, woman, and child in China, and during the festivals and holiday seasons, it was always served.

Chapter 24

When the New Year's holiday finally arrived, everyone was so excited, but Chen's worst fear came true. Along with their corn porridge, as part of the celebration, the guards served all the prisoners a good-sized bowl of boiled pork.

Chen dared not complain. How could he? The warden had gone to great effort to make this special meal for the prisoners. To be given such a meal was unimaginable with a famine and hard times sweeping China. Besides, he was in prison where prisoners could expect to receive nothing more than corn or rice porridge.

There was no special seasoning on the pork, and by the time the men received their portions, it was almost cold. Under ordinary circumstances, boiled pork might have seemed like boring fare, but for these half-starved prisoners, it was a feast, and they welcomed it with hand clapping and cheers.

But of course, Chen knew he could not eat the pork. Such a thing was forbidden by God in the Bible. Well-known verses of Scripture came to mind as he watched the guards dish up the pork. *"Swine . . . is unclean to you. Their flesh you shall not eat, and their carcasses you shall not touch. They are unclean to you"* (Leviticus 11:7, 8, NKJV). *"Do you not know that you are the temple of God and that the Spirit of God dwells in you?"* (1 Corinthians 3:16, NKJV).

Chen took the bowl of pork from the guard and sat staring at it. He was so hungry! All he could think of was the need to put something into his stomach other than the corn gruel they ate three times a day. Food with protein in it would be wonderful! His body needed it! His mind craved it! It seemed anything would be welcome—except this pork, of course. It could not be blessed by God even in this prison where there was so little to eat: even if the nourishment from this pork would keep him alive in a place where he was sure no one would care what he did, even if he had to die from lack of nutrition.

The moment was a surreal one. Chen stared at the bowl in his hands and saw that his hands were shaking. Was he weak from lack of food, or was he just scared he might fail this test of character? He looked down at his arms and saw they were thinner now than when he first came to the prison. He could feel his ribs under his dingy shirt and the foul-smelling winter underwear. He knew his health was deteriorating rapidly and realized just how serious lack of food could be in a place like this.

The cold of winter was becoming Chen's worst enemy now, and he feared it almost more than he feared this pork. What would happen to him as the temperatures dropped in the days ahead? How much longer could he last on the corn gruel rations? With so little food to eat, he was afraid his willpower would begin to break down. Would he give up his faith in God if that happened? Would he lack the strength to stand firm for his beliefs about things such as this pork?

The guard serving the meat caught the look of anguish and disappointment on Chen's face. "What's the problem?" he growled.

Chen snapped out of his melancholy mood and made his decision. It was now or never. He was ravenously hungry, but he would stand for the right! His hands were still weak. His body still shook from the cold. His stomach still growled as the meat stared up at him from the bowl. But it didn't matter. There was no doubt in his mind that if he honored God, the Lord would bless him for his faithfulness.

"I'm sorry. I can't eat the meat," Chen announced with conviction.

The guard glanced at Chen in surprise. "Why, what's wrong with it?"

"My God has asked that I not eat pork." Chen swallowed hard, and then hurried on. "In His Holy Book, God warns me that pork is not healthy for my body. It will contaminate my mind and defile my soul."

The other prisoners were already eating their bowls of pork with gusto, smacking their lips, rubbing their stomachs, and smiling at one another for a change. This was the best food they had eaten in months! But now at the sound of Chen's words, the place became quiet. Everyone stopped to stare at him in shock. Was he crazy? During hard times like this, regular citizens on the streets didn't get to eat this well. Pork would be a feast anywhere, the greatest of all delicacies in China! But here in this prison, a starving man was refusing to eat pork. He had to be out of his mind!

The guard finally found his voice. "Prisoners can't be choosers," he growled, echoing the thoughts of every inmate.

Chen bowed his head respectfully to the guard. "Thank you for your kindness, sir, but I have never eaten pork. You can give it to someone else. I'm sure they will appreciate it."

The guard stopped again to stare at Chen. He couldn't believe his ears! Not eat pork? He had never heard of anything so ridiculous in all his life! Everyone in China ate pork. It was the meat of choice everywhere! Yet here was a man refusing to eat it in prison where the prisoners were slowly starving to death from malnutrition.

The guard stood there a moment longer, not knowing what to do. Finally, he took the bowl from Chen's hands and walked out the gate of the jail cell. The prisoners remained motionless, their eyes wide with surprise at Chen as if he were a man with two heads. Not eat pork? Was he for real? They could not comprehend his logic or his decision. One by one they returned to the treat that had been set before them shaking their heads in disbelief.

What would become of this strange prisoner? they all wondered. Who would dare to refuse the greatest meal a warden could give his prisoners? The warden would clearly be offended and angry at this rejection of his gift, would he not? Surely Chen would be punished for it. Would they beat him? Would the warden make him go without food again for a day or two? Or worse! If pork wasn't good enough for him, would the warden think he didn't deserve to eat at all? If that happened, the preacher man would starve to death for sure.

However, a few minutes later, the guard came back again carrying another bowl in his hands. "We are sorry that you were not happy with the meat," the guard bowed respectfully to Chen. "The warden sends his compliments and would like you to have this instead." He handed the bowl to Chen.

When the guard left, the prisoners nearest Chen crowded around him to see what was in his bowl. "It's bean curds," one prisoner exclaimed. "Just bean curds. Tofu."

"I wish I had bean curds," another prisoner chimed in. "Chen's lucky. He has something no one else got."

"That's because he's a Christian and not afraid to be different," a third prisoner announced with admiration as he came to stand by Chen and look into the cup. "I wish I could be brave like you, Chen." And so the comments went, and by the time Chen had finished his bowl of tofu, there was a new level of respect for him in the prison; not just because he had stood up for his beliefs but also because he had made an impact on the prison officials. More men now crowded around Chen to ask him questions, and the angels smiled at Chen's new status of celebrity.

Little did Chen know the world of good he had done for his fellow prisoners. Hard times could be endured if one would dare to stand up for his convictions, and now, in a small way, these men understood the concept too. They had seen it with their own eyes. This incident had proved beyond a shadow of a doubt that Chen was a man of his word, and clearly, a man of God.

He could not know that his decision to turn down the pork would one day save him from punishment and great shame in this prison. For now, he would just enjoy his new status in the prison—and the bean curds, of course.

Chapter 25

The weeks passed by painfully, and the days began to blur together. Would he never get out of prison? Chen had been in "the cage" for nearly six long months now. Prisoners came and went, but always he was retained. At this point, only one old man had been in the prison longer than Chen.

Chen would never have managed to keep track of time had it not been for the number of marks he made daily with a pencil on the floor under his sleeping mat. It was a discouraging thing to have to do every day, but keeping a careful tally was the only thing that seemed to help him save his sanity. *Please Lord,* he prayed, *help me get through this ordeal one day at a time! I must be strong and faithful to You in this place!*

Often now, the prison officials called Chen into the interrogation chamber. With energy and determination they badgered him, intending, if possible, to force him to renounce his beliefs, but he always remembered why he had been imprisoned in the first place. "I cannot deny the reasons for my faith," he would tell the interrogator. "Jesus died for me, and for that I must be true to Him."

But in spite of his efforts to remain upbeat, the reality of Chen's situation was beginning to sink in. More and more he found himself slipping into depression. He was cold and hungry all the time. The bones in his body stuck out in every direction. His filthy clothes hung on him like a scarecrow's, and he knew he smelled awful! He had no real perspective on that any longer, since everything and everyone reeked of the latrine and body odor. But one thing he did know— he hadn't had a bath since he had arrived in September.

Where are You, Lord? Chen would pray desperately. *I've called and called on You for deliverance, but always You are silent. These prison walls are pressing in around me until I feel I'm going to be smothered from being cooped up for so long!*

One day a new man was admitted to the prison. He appeared to be a man of dignity and honor, and an intelligent one at that. Chen soon learned he was an ex-government official who didn't approve of the "methods" used by Chairman Mao's communist henchmen.

"Welcome to our world," Chen whispered the first chance he got. "I'm Chen."

"My name is Mr. Shi," the new man nodded respectfully.

Chen leaned in closer. "What are you in for?"

Mr. Shi held his head high. "I wouldn't agree to the interrogation of an elderly monk who was serving in a local Buddhist temple. He's a good old soul and never hurt a flea in his life. 'Why should I put him through that indignity?' I told them."

"And they didn't agree?" Chen raised his eyebrows.

Mr. Shi shook his head. "But given the chance again, I'd do the same."

It was nice to have a man of Mr. Shi's caliber in the prison. Chen could see they had much in common and hoped they would become good friends.

One afternoon a few days later, Shoushan, a young prisoner next to Chen in their cell, came back from the interrogation room all smiles. "I think the warden is going to let me go home pretty soon," he whispered excitedly as he sat down on his mat.

Chen glanced toward the guards, and then leaned toward Shoushan. His voice was barely audible as he mouthed the words, "I thought the warden didn't like you." Like the other prisoners, he had now mastered the technique of communicating without really talking. Facial expressions and hand gestures and words carefully mimed were all used effectively.

"He doesn't like me, it's true," Shoushan made a rattling sound in his throat. "He told me once he would see to it I never got out of here."

"So what makes you think you're going to get out now?"

"My family has been working with the warden to let me go." Shoushan's eyes brightened. "I think my father paid him some money."

"Did the warden tell you that?"

"He didn't say it, of course, but he was very nice to me, and when I see that, I know there's got to be some money changing hands somewhere. That's the way it goes around here. I've seen it too many times." He half smiled. "Mark my word. See if I'm right."

"I'm glad it's all working out for you," Chen smiled, though he had to admit to himself that he felt rather envious.

"Thanks, my friend." Shoushan laid a hand on Chen's shoulder. "And now I'd like to celebrate my good fortune with you. I have some good things to eat here." He glanced in the direction of the guards again, and then reached into a backpack lying beside him. "My family sent these, and the warden gave them to me today." He pulled out a cake, some pieces of candy, and several small packets filled with a sweet sticky rice dessert. "Would you like some?" he extended his

Chains in China

hand, offering Chen some of the sweet desserts.

Chen stared at the little rice packets. Sweet sticky rice was a favorite among the Chinese. He knew how precious they must be and the trouble Shoushan's family had gone through to get them to him. How could he take the treats from Shoushan even if the man was offering them?

"Thank you, Shoushan," he said slowly, "but I can't take your rice treats. I hope you're not offended. I'm sorry. It just wouldn't be right. They're a special gift from your family."

"OK." Shoushan smiled again. "Would you accept some pieces of candy, then?"

Chen hesitated. "All right, but only one piece. They're yours." He bowed his head respectfully. "I'm honored." It was only then that Chen noticed the other prisoners staring at him enviously. Getting to eat anything out of the ordinary in this prison was a rare experience, and it was clear they were jealous of Shoushan's gesture toward Chen.

"You must be a very special friend of his," a prisoner whispered to Chen. "I wish I were in your shoes."

Chen went to bed that night feeling better about his experience in the prison than he had in a long time. His undernourished body still shivered in the cold. His stomach still growled from the little bit of gruel they had given him in his metal cup, but Shoushan's candy somehow made up for it.

Thank You, Lord, for the unexpected things that make life sweet. Chen smiled up into the darkness. *You are so good to give me friends here in this prison, and the piece of candy. It is such a small thing, Lord, but with so little to look forward to, I am grateful.*

He slept well that night. The air was just as cold and the floor just as hard, but the warm friendship extended him by Shoushan had made a world of difference in his life.

The next morning, however, Chen awoke to real commotion in his cell.

"Someone's been going through my things!" Shoushan was shouting angrily. He was fumbling through his backpack pulling things out right and left, laying them on his sleeping mat. "My sticky rice desserts are gone!" he kept repeating. "Someone stole them while I was sleeping!"

A buzz of excitement ran through the prison cell, and the guards soon showed up. "What's all the racket about?" one of them demanded.

The prisoners crowded up against the cell bars. "A thief stole Shoushan's candy!" they all clamored at once. "Someone in here is a thief!" The rumble of voices began to build.

The men began to utter curses against the "thief," using all kinds of superstitious incantations. Some went to their own stash of personal possessions and drew out little boxes full of toenail and fingernail clippings. These could be used as superstitious fetishes to cast spells of bad luck on the supposed thief. Others glared around at the prisoners in the cell, shouting, "Four! Four!" hoping the guilty party would reveal himself with looks of fear and panic. *Four* is the most evil of numbers in Chinese culture, sure to bring bad luck at any time of day or night.

But the truth was that no one could really tell who had stolen the treats. Shoushan's sleeping mat was between Chen and Deming, another prisoner who had recently arrived at the prison. Little was known about Deming, but it was rumored he had been involved in a case of bribery and extortion at a bank.

A buzz of excitement continued to mount in the prison cell, and then suddenly died away as the prisoners turned to stare at Chen and Deming. It was likely that one of these two men was the guilty party. Not certain, but likely. The question was, Which one? They slept on either side of Shoushan, and both would have had easy access to Shoushan's backpack during the night when everyone was sleeping.

Chen knew this was a dangerous situation, one that could easily get out of hand in a prison. Criminals were usually put in prison because of the violent or dishonest things they had done in the outside world. Many of the men in the Wu Xi prison were rough and uncultured men from off the street. They were in the habit of taking what they wanted when they wanted it. It was ironic that the very thing they had done to others while living on the outside now angered them within the walls of this prison. If the whole thing hadn't been so serious, Chen might have smiled a bit at the hypocrisy of it all. Either way, the case of the stolen treats was now beginning to take on a rather symbolic significance of its own.

"Wait a minute!" Shoushan suddenly held up his hand. "I just thought of something." He looked into his backpack again, and then at Chen. "There was pork in those sticky rice balls. Chen doesn't eat pork. I know he wouldn't have stolen my sticky rice in the first place because he wouldn't eat it. He couldn't! The meat is forbidden by his God."

The truth of Shoushan's statement could not be denied. Everyone remembered that Chen had refused to eat the pork served on New Year's Day. He had been so hungry, but he had been true to his convictions. And if he was willing to do that for his God, he wouldn't steal the sticky rice treats for anything in the world! Especially not to eat them! He was too honest! He was too loyal to the principles of his God!

And now everyone turned their eyes on Deming. "So it was you!" they all chorused, and if looks could have killed, Deming would have been dead on his sleeping mat. "You are the evil one!" they shouted. "May evil come to haunt you all the days of your life!" and they all began throwing toenails and fingernails at him. It was a scary thing to see such hexes being thrown about. Chen was glad he wasn't the guilty one and that he had the protection of angels with him.

Deming cowered in fear as the curses and bad-luck fetishes rained down upon him, and it was plain to see he understood his fate. From that day forward, no one trusted the thief. He was ostracized from everyone in the prison. No one made contact with him anymore. No one ate with him. In fact, no one would even look at him. His plight was a sad one, pathetically so, almost as if he didn't exist.

It was clear that justice had been served. Chen had been vindicated. He had stood for the right by not eating the pork on New Year's Day, and his values had saved him in the end when he might have been unjustly accused of being a thief.

Chapter 26

Food supplies in many parts of China had greatly dwindled by now, due to the economic policies of communism set in place by Mao Zedong. Industry was suffering under the mismanagement of resources and workers. In the late 1950s, millions of unskilled peasants were taken from the farms to work the factories, leaving women and children to manage the new co-op farms. This in turn caused crop shortages, but the farm representatives in many districts were afraid to give the government the truth about crop yields.

As a result, the government syphoned off large stashes of grain based on the false production figures. Much of this surplus grain was used to repay loans they owed the Soviet Union; however, much of it rotted in warehouses in the cities where it was taken to be stored. Sadly, this program of mismanagement left the peasants too little to survive on. Even worse, the government prohibited people from leaving their farms to stabilize the economy, which doomed many to starvation.

And then, to make matters worse, during the spring and summer of 1960, China's economy was hit with an additional two-edged sword. Numerous floods hit some regions, while others suffered from the worst droughts in recent history. This caused even greater food shortages and the beginning of a widespread famine that would last for the next three years.

For all these reasons, food became very scarce, and the harsh temperatures of winter made the trauma even worse. People everywhere in China were so hungry they were eating every animal they could find, both domestic and wild—dogs, cats, rats. To survive, they had to eat creepy-crawly creatures such as worms and grasshoppers, and even grass and bark from trees.

The famine was getting so bad now in some towns that unless something drastic was done—and soon—every single person would die. Pain and suffering were widespread, with the effects cutting a swath across the length and breadth of China. In the end, it was said the losses reached at least thirty to forty million people.

Chen knew little of these statistics in the outside world. All he knew was his desperate need to survive in the Wu Xi prison. The winter days were getting longer, but the cold temperatures persisted. To Chen, now emaciated with hunger, it seemed life had come to a standstill. He began to lose his grip on reality and the need to stay alert. He was losing the compelling drive to witness for Jesus that had inspired him to be faithful when he first arrived at the prison.

Gone was the picture of health he had always valued so much in himself. His face was gaunt and thin, with dark rings around his eyes sunken into the sockets of his skull. His ribs looked like a washboard. His abdomen protruded grotesquely from the swelling of infected bowels due to the poor prison food. His legs were like beanpoles. His teeth began to loosen due to the lack of vitamins and nutrients in the food, and some days his teeth chattered so hard he was afraid they would fall out.

Would he ever live a normal life again? Would he ever get out of prison? And if he didn't, how long could he keep up his strength? Could he last for years in this place? It didn't seem likely. He had heard of prisoners in prison camps living for decades, but how they pulled off such feats of endurance was beyond him. It took a man with an iron will to make it in conditions like the ones found in the Wu Xi prison. Did a man's religion make a difference in how strong he could be in a place like this? Chen had always thought Christian prisoners could have an advantage, even though they were sometimes treated worse. At least their faith could give them peace of mind and a hope that God would pull them through.

But for Chen, the answers didn't seem that easy anymore. Pain and suffering were his closest companions. Some days he feared death would be his unavoidable enemy. Other days he almost wished it would be his friend. It was clear the Chinese government cared little about whether he lived or died. And why should they? All they wanted was to get a confession out of him or starve him to death in the process.

The food in the prison was as bad as it had ever been, only now there was less of it, if that was possible. Portions were getting smaller. He had grown accustomed to the same foul corn gruel offered at each meal, but that didn't make it any more nourishing. His clothes hung on him like a clothesline. Nights were long and hard on the cold floor. He had no books to read. Days were monotonous without a chance to talk openly to the other prisoners.

But Chen was not easily intimidated by the conditions and rules in this prison. As bad as they might seem, they did serve a positive purpose. He began to wonder if the restrictions imposed in his prison life might, in fact, be the very things that were giving him reasons for living. The energy it took to communicate on the sly with other prisoners was very frustrating and tedious at best. Having simple conversations about the food or weather or families of his fellow prisoners ended up being quite a chore.

When he wanted to share something with one of the inmates or ask them a question, he had to keep one eye on the guards at all times. Talking was forbidden. Prisoners were still being shackled as punishment for openly communicating with one another in the prison cell. Chen himself had been handcuffed for doing so, but only twice: once when he first arrived and once again when he and another prisoner had gotten into an argument about the personal space for their floor mats.

Chen's mat had now finally moved to the head of the line since he had been at the prison longer than anyone else. Some days he felt a great need to defend his claim to this spot farthest from the latrine, and other days it seemed to matter little. It was all so petty, really. The whole prison stank like a latrine! After being in this prison for so long, why should it matter where his mat lay? Chen had been so embarrassed the second time he was cuffed that he wouldn't speak to anyone for days.

He couldn't believe he had allowed himself to get upset over such a thing as the placement of his sleeping mat. And yet it shouldn't have been surprising. He valued his personal dignity. Besides his faith in God, personal dignity was the one thing that could get him through the endless days of tedium and pain. It was hard enough being in prison at all, let alone having to eat bad food and sleep on the crowded cement floor next to a putrid latrine.

But he was getting good at it. For him, staying alive in this place had become a science, if nothing else. The life he constructed for himself in prison must now encompass all the ways to survive, and that included out-thinking the guards. For instance, he had now learned that the best time to spend with fellow prisoners was when the officers left for a break or when there was a changing of the guard. It was at these times that Chen did most of his communicating with fellow inmates, and it always proved to be a source of bonding for them.

Sometimes the men talked about the lives of their family members on the outside. Sometimes they talked of what they would do when they got back home. Sometimes they talked about their regrets for having committed crimes, or maybe the anger and hopeless frustration they felt at having to be locked up at all.

It was on these occasions that Chen most felt the need to be a witness for Jesus. During these times, he knew the men would be a captive and willing audience. This jail was a perfect place to give prisoners a chance to review their past. Little did the warden know the favor Chen was doing him in helping to bring real changes to the lives of these men. It was the ideal place for them to search their hearts and visualize a better life for themselves in the future.

And the gospel story often fit into those conversations. It didn't matter what the topic might be. Whatever the issue, Chen always managed to slip in some good news about salvation and the Bible.

When the men felt depressed and alone without a friend in the world, Chen would recite Bible verses for them. "In the day of my trouble I will call upon You, for You will answer me" (Psalm 86:7, NKJV). "[God] has loved you with an everlasting love," he would tell the men, "therefore with lovingkindness [He has] drawn you" (Jeremiah 31:3, NKJV). And then there was Acts 16:31: "Believe on the Lord Jesus Christ, and you will be saved," Chen would tell them (NKJV), and with pathos in his voice, he would add, "Why would you not believe in such a God?"

The promises Chen quoted from the Bible seemed to help the prisoners because they offered courage and hope. Always he gave them a perspective that made them think, touching on something they perhaps had not thought about before. And it was these times that helped Chen make it through just one more day.

Mr. Shi seemed especially receptive to the Bible truths, and Chen was not really surprised. The man was intelligent and respectable. Hadn't he been brought to this prison because of his compassion for an old monk? Hadn't he already shown godly traits of character by his willingness to defend a man the government cared nothing about?

"God will reward you for your goodness," Chen told Mr. Shi. "The things we suffer in this world are nothing compared to the blessed home God is preparing for us in heaven. 'Eye has not seen, nor ear heard, nor have entered into the heart of man the things which God has prepared for those who love Him' " (1 Corinthians 2:9, NKJV).

"I believe," Mr. Shi said quietly. "You asked us why we would not believe in such a God, and I am here to say, I believe. It is the most logical thing I have ever said."

"Praise God," Chen could feel a lump growing in his throat. "God has brought you to this place in your life, Mr. Shi. Who knows, but that He may have arranged for us to come to this prison so we could meet."

"I believe that, too," Mr. Shi bowed his head. "I think I probably would not have listened to a Christian such as you on the outside." His voice trembled. "May God bless you, my brother Chen, for accepting His call to serve in this prison."

Chen bowed his head respectfully too. "And may the God of our fathers draw you close with cords of love when you grow discouraged and lonely," he said.

Chapter 27

Chen's body was racked with pain now pretty much every day. When he first came to the prison, his body had withstood the rigors of a poor diet. He had managed well enough under disgustingly unsanitary conditions. He had kept his mind strong through meditating on verses of Scripture and praying. Even the warden had been on Chen's prayer list.

But the health of Chen or his fellow inmates was of little concern to the warden. The prisoners had committed crimes against the Chinese communist government, and for this they must pay. Some he beat, many he interrogated relentlessly, and all were starved into cooperation.

And of all his prisoners, Chen was the guiltiest of them all, or so it appeared to everyone in the prison. Why else would the warden keep Chen in the place so long? The warden had been told to get a confession of guilt out of Chen, and that was what he intended to do.

The first time Chen had been interrogated, he had been accused of working for the counter-revolution and had clearly suffered for it with every indignity the warden could devise. Since that time, he'd had many sessions with government officials in the interrogation chamber, and the results were always the same. Chen maintained his devotion to his country, his innocence of any crime, and his great love for Jesus who had died for him.

The interrogators increased the number of sessions with Chen now; sometimes he faced several sessions in one week. Sometimes government representatives from Shanghai would question him, and when they grew tired, the warden would take over. The officials had been successful in "reforming" every other prisoner who had come through the prison, but Chen was of a different sort. It annoyed them that they had not been able to "break" him, as they called it. What kind of man was this who would rather sit in prison and starve than give up his faith in his God? He was nothing but skin and bones now, a mere shadow of the man they had arrested the previous fall. Without a doubt, Chen was the most "stubborn, willful" prisoner they had ever processed in the Wu Xi prison.

It was a heartless charade! Chen was a good man, patient under fire, enduring the accusations hurled his way, but that didn't seem to make any difference to the officials. Each bout with Chen was seen as a personal challenge for all of them, especially for the warden. With every added round of questions, he grew more determined and more relentless in his efforts to conquer the Christian pastor. Getting Chen to give up his Christian beliefs would be the warden's greatest triumph.

It was now clear to Chen that the prison officials intended to ruin him physically and mentally, and if need be, starve him into submission. But Chen was a strong man mentally. Breaking him down psychologically was proving to be a much harder task than they had thought it would be, even though his body was greatly weakened. He had now withstood the worst they could give him for nearly seven months.

But stubbornly hanging on seemed futile for Chen. Worse would come. Everyone knew what the eventual sentence would be for Chen's "crimes" if he would not submit. It was common talk among the prisoners.

"They'll send you to a stone quarry," Anguo whispered one morning as they were sitting around after breakfast. Anguo had recently arrived at the prison, one in a family of four brothers who had resisted the government programs being promoted in Mao's Zedong's Great Leap Forward. His latest crime had been staging secret meetings in Wu Xi to find a way to get one of his younger brothers out of a work camp.

"At the quarry they work you like horses without any feed." Anguo's eyes darted warily toward the guards. "I had another older brother doing hard labor in one of those camps for eight years before they let him out. He looked so old and worn from all the mistreatment, we didn't even recognize him. Now they're after the rest of us." Chen could tell by the angry lines on Anguo's face that he was going to be in this prison for a very long time.

"The quarries are like death camps," said another prisoner, "but the mines are even worse! They send you down into the belly of the earth, and you never see the sun again. Work starts way before sunrise, and you come back up after it's dark." His face clouded over. "It's awful! You kind of go crazy not being exposed to the sun or anything! My father did it for years. With no sun and breathing all that coal dust, he just wasted away."

"It's true." Anguo made a fist and pounded it in the palm of his hand. "But I'd still rather be there than here! If I had a choice, I think I'd rather serve ten years of hard labor in a mine or prison quarry than one year in this cage."

"He's right! We're with you!" the rest of the prisoners echoed.

Chen had mixed feelings about that kind of talk. Living in this cage was difficult, but ten years in a stone quarry seemed like forever! He shivered at the prospect of a prison sentence like that. The thought of such a fate made him grow weak in the knees, and he felt himself slipping into depression again. Was God going to allow such a thing to happen to him? *I've got to snap out of this!* Chen scolded himself. *This kind of attitude is what's going to kill me.* What was it his father used to say? *"In the great controversy between good and evil, bad things sometimes happen to godly people."* That made sense, and it was to be expected for anyone who claimed to be a follower of Christ. Lots of Bible characters had suffered the kind of treatment Chen was getting in this prison—and worse. Why should he complain? Joseph, Jeremiah, and Peter had all spent time in prison. Was he any better than they?

And was he too good to be treated as Jesus was treated? Surely suffering for Jesus was the highest of all honors, and that was good enough for Chen. He felt ashamed of himself now for letting his faith in God slip. *"The Lord is my rock and my fortress and my deliverer,"* he reminded himself for the umpteenth time since he had arrived in the prison (2 Samuel 22:2, NKJV), and then smiled as he realized he had just given himself a much-needed spiritual pep talk.

The early days of spring were here now. The days grew longer and the air was warming. Through the open slots high along the prison wall, Chen could see branches of the trees getting ready to bud. He could hear birds outside now and then, and it cheered his heart to listen to their happy songs. His spirits rose with the exuberance of spring, and he felt sure now that things would get better for him. He had done his time and paid his debt. He had made it through the long winter, and the government officials would respect him for that. Any day now, they would come to let him out.

But that was about as far as Chen got with his emotional high. Within a matter of minutes, he always came crashing down to the realities of prison life. He stared around him at the other prisoners in the "cage." Everybody looked awful! The famine in China had brought on a shortage of food everywhere, especially in this prison, bringing all forms of malnutrition upon the men. Some suffered from anemia, some from rickets, and some from scurvy. The men were now so weak from sickness and lack of food that it was difficult to keep from shivering even in the spring air, warmer though it was during the day.

Chen was beginning to lose his appetite. Something had changed inside of him. He was finding it hard to digest the little bit of gruel they were being given, and the cough he had developed earlier in the winter had now gone deep into his chest. He knew that was a bad sign for a man in a place like this.

And then one of the prisoners died—maybe from hunger, maybe from the cold, maybe from disease. No one could say why exactly, but Chen was sure it must be a combination of all three. The man was old. He was bent with years and broken from months of poor food and appalling prison conditions. As the guards carried him out on a stretcher, Chen and the others watched in silence. The old man's eyes were closed in death, but his face was still pinched with pain. It was sad to think that a man's life had been wasted here in this deplorable prison. And for what?

The man's death haunted Chen. He couldn't get the poor man out of his mind. Would he suffer a similar fate? He didn't want to think of such a thing, but even death was a possibility in God's plan for a man's life. That's the way it was sometimes in a sinful world. Was God's work for Chen finished in this prison now? Would he soon be laid to rest like this unfortunate prisoner being carried out on a stretcher? Sometimes Chen thought death would not be such a bad thing. If he were to stay in prison, there wasn't much of a life to look forward to anyway.

Chapter 28

But Chen knew this was not a good attitude to have, and it certainly wouldn't help him keep his spirits up if he intended to be a help to the prisoners in his cell. He had had many conversations with other prisoners to cheer them up, but today was a day he needed someone to help him get over the hump.

"Don't give up!" Mr. Shi told Chen. "You are a strong man emotionally. Your God will save you to see the outside of this prison again."

Chen was encouraged by Mr. Shi's words, and he felt ashamed that this man who wasn't even a Christian was having to remind him to trust in God. And Mr. Shi was right! God did have a plan! The angels were with him in this prison. The Holy Spirit was giving him comfort, and no matter what happened, he was confident Jesus would not forsake him. *Thank You, Lord*, was his most frequent and heartfelt prayer now. *I owe You my life.*

A few days later, the warden came down to the main cell block with an announcement to the prisoners. "Men, we're going to give you a special treat," he said with a twinkle in his eye. "You're all going to the showers."

Chen could hardly believe it. A shower? It had been so long since he had taken a bath or a shower, he wasn't even sure he knew what a shower was anymore. He hadn't bathed since the day he had walked into the Wu Xi prison the previous September. "Well, I guess there's always a first time for everything," Chen joked.

Water was a scarce commodity in this place, they were told, so washing up was rare. Not surprisingly, everyone smelled like they belonged in a barnyard! The food smelled bad enough, but the men's clothes had never been washed, so that made it even worse. Every crack and pore and crevice in the prison seemed to reek with the horrific odors of the place.

"Prisoners in cells one to four may go first," announced the warden, as he signaled the guard to open their gate. The men were so happy! If they'd had the energy, they would have skipped for joy down the corridor. But with such little food to nourish them, even going to the showers was exhausting. Most of the men were so weak from malnutrition that the strong ones had to help the weak

123

ones to the showers. If Mr. Shi hadn't helped him, Chen would never have even made it.

Like the rest of the prisoners, Chen's muscles had atrophied from lack of exercise. He had always been such a strong young man, but now he had almost no muscle left. It was no more than thirty meters to the showers, but his legs were so weak, he felt like a leaf shaking in the wind. He couldn't even control his feet to make them go where he wanted to go!

It was such a relief for the prisoners to get their moldy old clothes off, but Chen couldn't believe the emaciated condition of all the prisoners. Most of the men looked like walking skeletons. Even the lice crawling on them were having a hard time surviving. But Chen himself was in the worst condition of all. Every rib was showing. His arms and legs looked like toothpicks. His cheekbones were protruding from his face, and his skull had lost much of its hair.

When the water was turned on and the men first felt it cascading down upon their bodies, many began to cry. For so long they had imagined what it would be like to take a shower or bath, and now that the moment was here, they could not bear it emotionally. And Chen was no different. Every nerve in his body tingled with excitement to be touched by the water, and for a minute, he thought he must be in heaven! It was a moment never to be forgotten.

The nights were warmer now, and by the marks on the floor under his mat, Chen knew spring had fully come. There were other signs of spring too. All morning, birds flew in and out of the open spaces above the cage, bringing twigs and other materials to build their nests up under the roof. Afternoons, he could feel the fresh air blowing in above him doing its best to replace the foul prison air below. At night, he could hear the crickets chirping out their little songs, serenading him as he slept.

Chen was like a walking corpse these days and weighed less than seemed possible for a man. He had been in the prison for nearly eight months, but it seemed more like eight years. His joints ached, he had abdominal cramps now nearly every day, and his cough was getting worse than ever. And still he lived. Would this tortuous ordeal never end?

He lay on his crusty old sleeping mat most days now, too exhausted to do much else. He was so tired! He was so broken! He had been hoping every day that the warden would have mercy on him and become the humanitarian he claimed to be. He had been praying that the prison officials would reconsider their program of indoctrination for him, that they would do the right thing and let him go home. He had suffered enough!

But now he was beginning to have thoughts of a different nature. He was beginning to fear that God might be asking him to accept a different fate than freedom. Was it possible God was asking him to die a martyr's death? The thought was new for him, and it frightened him to contemplate such things. He was not frightened by the thought of death but by the reality that maybe God was not going to rescue him after all, as he had been expecting all along. He had had his doubts often enough, but he had always come back to the confidence of promises from Scripture that God would deliver him as he had Jonah in the belly of the whale, the three Hebrews in the fiery furnace, and Daniel in the lions' den.

On another level, though, it seemed almost euphoric that he might be able to escape this prison death trap. If that was part of God's plan to bring the gospel to the hardest of the hard hearts in this prison, then Chen was willing. Was there a guard or prisoner in this place who might surrender his life to God because he had witnessed Chen's testimony of suffering? Certainly such a thing would make his death worth the sacrifice. Even death would have its reward in the eternal salvation of a Chinese brother.

And then one morning Chen awoke with a bad headache and a fever. No one could be surprised at such a turn of events, least of all Chen. However, the strange feelings coming over him this time were of a different sort. He couldn't remember ever having felt quite like this before. It was a wonder he had made it through the winter at all. God had been good to him keeping him alive, and he knew there had to be a reason for that, but now an ominous feeling began to creep over him. It was a strange kind of feeling deep down inside of him, and he couldn't shake it. He was in trouble and he knew it.

When Chen took his turn at the latrine, he almost fainted with pain, and then noticed he was bleeding. "This is serious!" Mr. Shi frowned as he helped Chen wash up. "We need to get you to the doctor!"

They sat together waiting for medical help, and that was an encouragement to Chen. Mr. Shi was a true friend indeed. "Your God whom you serve will not abandon you," Mr. Shi said quietly. "He has been caring for you here in this prison. He has kept you alive. That much I know. Take courage, Chen. The Lord preserved your life all these months for a reason. He will not abandon you now. I would have never heard the ways of Christianity and truths of the Bible if it had not been for you, and for this I am eternally grateful, my brother."

The guards had to come into the cell to get Chen because he could hardly walk. He was so doubled up with pain that he had to stop and grab the prison bars to catch his breath every few seconds. With great difficulty, he managed to hobble down the prison corridor and into the infirmary before collapsing into a chair.

The prison doctor gave Chen an injection of penicillin, but it didn't seem to help him any. He remained under the doctor's watchful eye for several days, but still he had a fever and pain, and still he bled. It appeared the prison doctor could do nothing for him, and so the warden was called in.

After the warden had examined Chen, he and the doctor went into another room. Chen couldn't hear their conversation well, but he could hear bits and pieces of an angry argument. "He stays!" the warden shouted.

"I don't think you understand just how serious his condition is," the doctor was saying in hushed tones.

"I don't care how serious it is!" the warden kept on. "He's not leaving, I tell you! I need a confession out of that man!" And then a door slammed.

The next morning, though, the doctor came to talk with Chen. "I'm sending you to the Wu Xi village hospital," he said with downcast eyes.

"What's wrong with me?" Chen asked hopefully.

"I can do nothing more for you here," was all the doctor would say. "You are very sick."

After the doctor left, Chen lay on his bed in the examination room looking at the ceiling. So they were going to send him to a regular hospital. *My disease must be serious,* he thought. *If it wasn't, they wouldn't be taking me to the city hospital.*

Chains in China

Chapter 29

Later that morning, four prisoners came with a stretcher. They gently lifted Chen onto it, and then under guard carried him out through the front doors of the prison. Chen's head was buzzing now from an intense fever that was getting worse, and yet, strangely enough, his mind seemed clear.

As the men carried him down the street toward the hospital, Chen seemed to be in the most vivid of dreams. He was tired and every bone ached, but he didn't want to miss a thing—the green leaves, the white clouds, the blue sky. It was wonderful to smell the freshness of spring! It was magnificent having the warm sun roll over him like the waves of an ocean surf at sunset. For almost nine months, the prisons walls had cut him off from direct sunlight, and now its glorious rays seemed sent from heaven to heal his soul.

He watched the little sparrows flitting from branch to branch in the trees along the roadway to the hospital. They seemed so happy and alive and free. It was a surreal feeling for Chen, and he felt as if he was one with the birds, as though he, too, was being set free.

Secretly, he hoped he might see some of his church members by chance along the way to the hospital. That would be a real treat! If they had known he was coming this way, he felt sure they would have made plans to meet and greet him as he passed in the street. Maybe they would find out where he was and come to see him now that he was going to be in the public hospital.

The next day when Chen woke up, he couldn't remember anything from the day before. And he couldn't remember where he was. Had he been dreaming? Everything seemed to be a fog in his memory now. The prison. The starvation rations. The desperately foul conditions. The interrogations. Had it all been part of some horrible nightmare?

Then he saw all the hospital beds with sick men around him in the room, and he remembered. He was ill. Very ill, according to the doctor. For a moment, he wanted to panic. He broke into a sweat, and his heart began to race. But then he remembered he was a pastor and a son of the Living God. He had a purpose in life. If he was alive, God must still have work for him to do, and that thought encouraged him greatly.

"What are you in for? You look awful!" A small bald-headed man in one of the beds nearest Chen was staring at him. "My name is Deli," he added and gave Chen a toothy grin.

"What am I doing here?" Chen half smiled. That was a big question for him. He was sick, yes, but was that the full answer? In God's world, one could never be sure of all the reasons. However, one thing was sure: in this hospital bed, he would find another perfect opportunity to let his light shine for Jesus. Here was a captive audience. Here in this hospital room were a dozen men who weren't going anywhere. Like Chen, they were bound to beds of sickness. Maybe God had brought them here for such a time as this, to hear the good news of the gospel story.

Help me say the right things, Chen prayed as he realized the gift he had been given.

"I'm very sick," he began. "I've been in prison, and the doctor at the prison was afraid I might die if he didn't send me here. I'm a Seventh-day Adventist pastor," he turned his head on his pillow to look at Deli and the other men. "I'm a Christian leader here in the community, and I've been studying the Bible with folks who are interested. The government has asked that I stop talking about my beliefs, but I cannot. I love God too much, and I want to serve Him."

"Aren't you afraid of the government?" Deli's eyes were wide. "I know I would be. They don't allow such things."

Chen thought for a moment. "I'm afraid at times, yes. The government says it is against the law to speak of these things, but I must obey Jesus. Jesus is always with me. His angels give me courage when I am at my weakest and most discouraged."

"Who is this Jesus?" Deli continued, pressing the questions. "And who are the angels?"

"I think I can say it best this way," Chen squinted at the men now sitting up in their beds and taking notice. "Jesus is the Son of God. He came to this world to die for our sins. And angels are God's supernatural warriors sent from heaven to help us on our earthly journey."

"This is true?" Deli stared at Chen, unable to comprehend such information. "This is something all Christians believe?"

Chen nodded. "What I tell you is the truth. I believe it in here," Chen pointed to his head, "and in here," he pointed at his heart. "But more importantly, I live it, and because of this, I must serve my God. He has said that I must tell everyone the good news of salvation, that He loves all men and is coming soon to save us from the troubles of this world. 'For God so loved the world that He gave His only begotten Son, that whoever believes in Him might have eternal life' [John 3:16, NKJV].

"I wish I had my Bible with me. Then I would read you the words of Jesus Himself." Chen swallowed with emotion as he watched the faces of these men who were listening so intently. "I am so excited about this good news that I must share it with everyone I meet. That's why I am willing to suffer anything to be faithful to my God. I cannot stop talking about Him."

He bowed his head as if in submission to his heavenly mission. "And that is why I have been in prison for the last year," he added. "It is why I am so desperately sick. It is why I am now here in this hospital with you. They have tried to stop me by interrogating me and threatening me. They have tried to starve me into submission, but Jesus has kept me alive to tell the story of His love and His plan to save all men. I cannot stop even if they kill me, because Jesus Himself has asked me to bring the gospel story to you." Chen glanced around at all the men again. "The good news I want to share is that Jesus died for you. He died for me. We are all children of the heavenly Father."

It was so quiet in the hospital room that one could have heard a pin drop. Every eye was on Chen as he lay on his hospital bed. The sunshine coming through the window warmed his face with the light of heaven, it seemed, and the men were in awe of him, to put it simply. If what he was telling them was true, then it was the most incredible news they had ever heard. It was, in fact, too amazing for words! The Chinese government was guilty of putting people in prison for being Christian, but these men had never met one who was so cheerful about having to suffer for his faith.

Deli finally broke the silence. "Everything you say must be true then, or you would not risk so much to share this gospel, as you call it." He glanced around at the other men. "If this Jesus would die for us, as you say He did, then He must surely love us." He shook his head in disbelief. "It is more than I can comprehend."

A doctor came that afternoon to examine Chen. He looked into Chen's mouth and examined his eyes. He listened to his heart. He ran his hand over Chen's swollen abdomen but said nothing. Chen knew his condition was serious. The silence of every doctor who treated him said it all. It was why he was still in the hospital.

The doctor was making marks on a clipboard in his hands. "Have you ever had pneumonia?" he asked. "Have you had emphysema or bronchitis? How about tuberculosis?" He glanced at Chen over the rims of his glasses.

"I have always been in good health," Chen assured him. "I have never smoked or drunk alcohol, and I don't use drugs of any kind. But I am very sick now, as you can see. Tell me the truth, Doctor. Do I have one of those diseases you are talking about? Am I going to be all right?"

But the doctor would not answer Chen's questions. He only gave him some pills and some medicine to drink and then went away.

The doctor came back the next day and the next, but each time he went away, he would give Chen no answers one way or the other about his health. At one point, the warden must have showed up too, because Chen could hear the two of them arguing, just like the warden had done with the doctor in the prison.

Finally, on the fourth day in the Wu Xi hospital, the doctor spoke his mind. "You are a very sick man, Chen! I have done everything I can to stop your bleeding, but I have failed!" he said emphatically. "And yet you are still alive!" He shook his head as though Chen were a puzzle to solve. "I cannot understand why you are still alive."

On the morning of the fifth day, the doctor sent Chen back to prison. He had no cure for Chen but was afraid to say so, and Chen guessed it was because he feared his patient might give up and die on him there in the hospital. The Chinese had wanted to break Chen along with all the other prisoners, but it was against their code of ethics to kill a man in the process. *Very strange,* thought Chen. Starving a man was considered permissible in a prison, but starving him to death was off limits. A very strange philosophy indeed!

Chapter 30

Chen felt like the lowest of the low as he went back to cell number four in the prison. He had a splitting headache constantly now, and his fever was just as bad as ever. Sometimes he almost thought his head would explode from the pain.

At this point, he was certain his condition must be fatal, and he felt oddly resigned to the fact. When he closed his eyes, it was easy to think about what it would be like to die. That was clearly the direction in which he was headed, and he had the strange sensation of just wanting to get it over with.

That same afternoon, the prison guards came to "the cage" to take Chen to another jail cell. "I will miss you," Mr. Shi said bravely as he watched Chen go. "You have been more than a brother to me, and I will never forget your kindness." There were tears in his eyes. "You gave me the hope of heaven when I had nothing else."

Chen prayed with Mr. Shi from his stretcher, and the moment was a touching one. Here was a man of the world being touched by a man of God. The angels recorded the moment, knowing it would probably be the last time these two men would see each other in this life.

Chen's new surroundings were smaller but more inviting. Cage number seven was warmer and had only eight prisoners. Chen soon realized it was the prison infirmary, but most of the patients still had to lie on mats on the concrete floor. The best part was that in this cell there was more space and more freedom to move. Now everyone could stretch out and sleep well.

The next day, the warden came to Chen's cell and asked if he wanted to write his family a letter. "I'd like you to have a chance to meet your people once again," he said almost kindly. The warden helped him write the letter to someone of his choice, and Chen chose the church folks in Wu Xi. His mother and father lived too far away to help him at the moment, and he felt sure they would have no money to come see him anyway. The letter was an invitation for his church members to come to the prison to see him, but Chen was not putting his hopes on any of this. He had written letters to family and friends before, and little had ever come of it, except the long underwear he had received in December. His letters had been rewritten perhaps to say only what the warden wanted them to say.

Chen had to admit he was surprised at the kind words and treatment he was receiving from the warden, but he was worried too. The prison officials had always been slow to let the inmates write letters home. Why they were letting him write a letter now was a bit of a mystery. *Maybe the warden is not such a bad man after all,* Chen thought. *Maybe he is indeed a humanitarian as he claims.*

"Thank you," was all Chen could say, but after the warden left, another prisoner came to sit down beside Chen.

"They are going to let you go home," he announced confidently. "In three to four days, the warden will release you. Happens every time. If a sick prisoner in your condition receives permission to write home, it means the warden wants the family to come get him because his disease is so severe. This is a normal procedure in prisons for men who will soon die," he added.

Chen stared at the other prisoner suspiciously. The fog of confusion in his mind brought on by the fevered headache was keeping him from comprehending the enormity of what the man was saying.

"You are lucky," another prisoner added. "You may die, but at least you get to die free."

"Thanks," Chen heard himself say, but the envious looks everyone was giving him seemed so out of place. Here he was now virtually sentenced to die, and the other prisoners were telling him he was lucky. Chen had to think about that. He had been so miserable in the prison, and it was true he sometimes wished he could die. But lucky? He could hardly think of himself as being lucky to die. The idea of it all seemed so wrong, for the sake of the church, if for no one else. If he died, how could he continue to be a witness for God?

Chen wrote the letter asking for a relative or church worker to come meet with the warden. The fact that the prison officials seemed so anxious to get rid of him hadn't really hit home for him yet, but it didn't really matter much. He was so desperately sick. Even the thoughts of freedom running through his head didn't seem very logical anymore.

The thought of getting to go home was exciting, but the notion that he was going home to die made him feel desperate at best. He wasn't ready to die! There was still so much for him to do for God! He couldn't believe that this was heaven's plan for him, and one feeling more than any other kept running through his head. If God had preserved him this long, why would He let him die now, either inside the decrepit prison or outside its walls?

And then a new thought struck Chen. What if the other prisoners were wrong? What if the warden was just toying with him? What if the official had no intention of sending him home at all but was using yet another form of Chinese torture? *This is my last chance,* thought Chen. *If they don't let me go now, I will die in this prison for sure!*

Help me, Lord, he found himself praying again and again after he gave the letter to the warden. *I want to live! Help me escape this horrible nightmare!*

Two days passed, and Chen was beginning to wonder if the warden had forgotten about him again. He was spitting up blood now—lots of it—and he still had a severe headache and stomach cramps, but they were feeding him better. Now, instead of just one bowl of the corn meal gruel, they were giving him two. And yet, he was weak—so weak that he couldn't stand on his own to visit the latrine, and one of the other prisoners in the infirmary even had to help feed him.

Hope began to die again in Chen's heart. He couldn't last much longer. It was only a matter of days now, maybe hours, and he would be dead. In spite of the change in treatment and the move to another, larger prison cell, he knew no one in the prison system really cared what happened to him. No one from his family or church had ever been allowed to come see him. All he had ever had in this despicable place was God.

And now the thought of being set free didn't really seem to matter to Chen anymore. Whether released from prison or dead to this world, he would be free. He was only glad that the angels had been with him through this long ordeal. He was grateful that the Holy Spirit had come to give him the assurance he needed through the cruel months of torture and deprivation. He had been faithful to Jesus and done his part as God's witness in this prison full of derelicts and criminals. Heaven could ask nothing more.

Stay with me, Lord, Chen prayed. *When You are here with me in this prison cell, I have the peace of heaven with me, and that is all I need.*

On the afternoon of the third day, the warden finally came to the infirmary, and a spark of hope once again lit itself in Chen's heart. Would this be the day of his final deliverance? he wondered.

"Gather up your few belongings and follow me," the warden said quietly.

Chen was stronger today for some reason, and to his surprise, he was able to stand on his own, though the guards had to help him walk through the corridors to the prison holding room. Standing at the front gate were two young people from the Adventist church in Wu Xi—a woman and man. He recognized their faces, yet could not remember their names. Who were they? The warden was telling Chen they had come to take him home, but was it true?

And then he remembered. It was Chow and Enlai, her brother. Chen was ecstatic to see them and didn't know whether to laugh or cry. He had lived with these people and their family for a year when he first arrived in town, and they had treated him like a son. The memories of those days seemed like a dream now, but it was coming to him more clearly with every passing second.

Chow and Enlai were shocked at Chen's pitiful condition. Chow gasped and then burst into tears at the sight of their beloved pastor, now a mere skeleton of his former self. Chen's eyes were dark and sallow, sunken into a skull with almost no hair. His arms and legs were like toothpicks, and his ribs looked like a washboard.

His clothes hung limply on him, hardly disguising the condition of his emaciated body. He was wearing a ragged shirt, long underwear, and trousers that looked grimy and smelled like a cesspool. Except for the one shower allowed them during the early spring months, Chen had been wearing these same clothes continually since the day he had arrived the previous fall.

Chapter 31

Chen stood dumbfounded at the thought of finally going free! This was the moment he had dreamed of for so long now, and he wanted to savor every detail of it. The sunshine streaming through the front gate. The fresh smell of free air bringing everything to life in his nostrils. The deep love and care he saw on the faces of his church friends.

The reality of the moment finally caught up with him, however. The emotions of the moment were too much, and Chen suddenly broke down and began to weep. Great heaving sobs of grief and relief shook his frail scarecrowlike frame. He had been in this prison of death for more then ten months with nothing but a skeleton of skin and bones to show for it. And now he was finally going home.

Chow and Enlai asked the warden if they could carry Chen's things for him, but the warden only shrugged. Chen had nothing in this world he could call his own—no books, no personal identification papers, no clothes except the foul smelling ones on his back. Not wanting to send him away empty-handed, the warden handed him a coupon book with food rations in it.

"You are a normal person now, and I am a good man to let you go," the warden announced in the same arrogant tone he had used so many months before, when Chen first came to the prison. He pulled himself up to his full five feet six inches of height. "That is why I am sending you away with gifts," he added. "No one can call me less than a humanitarian."

Chen could only listen in wonder at the warden's lines of propaganda. It was a pitiful attempt on his part, but to Chen it was a ridiculous oxymoron of the greatest magnitude. He would have smiled at the ridiculous charade if he hadn't been so weak. After all the inhuman treatment of mental torture and starvation he had received in this place, the warden still wanted the title of humanitarian. It was all so pathetic! The man could not see himself for who he really was! He had put a perfectly good citizen into prison for being a Christian, all in the name of culture and government policy. If Chen hadn't become desperately sick unto death, they might have kept him in prison all his life.

But Chen knew the truth, and so did everyone else standing at the gate, visitors and guards alike. This warden would never be anything but a monster. Chen's only regret was that he had never managed to touch the officer's stony heart, no matter how much he'd prayed for him.

"Thank you," was all Chen would allow himself to say. He wanted to add, "Hope to see you around," but he knew it would be a lie.

The three of them walked out through the front gate, leaving Chen's horrible nightmare behind. Chen could hardly believe his good fortune, if one could call it that. He was finally out of prison, something he had given up hope would ever happen. God had been with him in prison, and there had been a Divine purpose for him to suffer through these long, hard months. That's all that mattered now.

Though Chen could not say he had converted the hearts of any guards, he had touched the lives of some prisoners. He knew that Mr. Shi, in particular, had come to know Jesus, and that had been an act of God. Deli, too, had heard the story of salvation. His life had been touched and changed through Chen's testimony, as had the lives of the other men in Deli's hospital ward. These men had been receptive, and Chen now prayed that come what may, they would be faithful to God until Jesus should come. Who could say what tender plants these seeds of the gospel story might grow for the church?

The trip across town to the home of church members was not a long one, but it was difficult for Chen. He could not walk, of course, and had to be carried there on an ox cart. As he rode along the bumpy streets, a seesaw of emotions again swept over him. He was so happy to be free, but he was also bitter about the wasted months he had spent in that horrible prison. He was grateful to God for getting him finally released, but the fact that he would die now was a reality. The warden had pushed him too far. His body was too weak from disease and malnutrition. Cases like his were hopeless. He could tell by the way people were looking at him when they passed the ox cart in the streets.

And yet Chen wanted peace more than anything in his moment of triumph. He wanted God's blessing in his life, and he made a conscious effort to keep his mind on the promises of God for those who have taken up their cross to follow Jesus. *"One thing I do: forgetting what is behind and straining toward what is ahead, I press on toward the goal to win the prize for which God has called me heavenward in Christ Jesus"* (Philippians 3:13, 14, NIV). Those words of Scripture seemed to express exactly how Chen felt right now, and they brought him real comfort.

When he arrived at Chow and Enlai's home, all his beloved church members came to see him. They prayed with him and thanked God for his deliverance from prison. They fed him some warm cabbage soup, but not too much because they knew it would be a shock to his frail system. The soup tasted better than Chen remembered anything could taste after eating corn meal gruel for a year. They gave him a soft mattress to sleep on for the night, but they knew they could not keep him long in Wu Xi. He was in very bad condition now and could die any time. His family would want to see him. That's why they took him to the train station after two days. Much as they wanted to keep their beloved pastor in Wu Xi and care for him, they knew it wasn't fair. His mother and father deserved to be with him in his final hours.

They put on a good show at the train station, wishing Chen well with many tears and fond wishes, reminding him to come see them soon. But Chen knew the truth. They were sending him home to die.

The trip to Lishui, his hometown, was difficult for a man who was so sick. He was coughing up blood now almost constantly, and he still had severe stomach cramps and a splitting headache. He could eat every very little of the hot soup his Wu Xi family had sent him because of internal pain. He didn't have an ounce of fat on him and had almost no muscle left to give him padding for the hard wooden benches of the train seats. No position, either sitting or lying down, brought him relief during the long hours of the journey. The excruciating pain he felt as the train stopped and started up again in every little town was almost more than he could bear, but there was no other way. There was nothing he could do to change the traveling conditions. He had to get home.

There was no one to help Chen in his greatest time of need. He was all by himself. He wished that someone could have made the trip with him, but times were hard, and there was no money for a second train ticket. Again, he was tempted to doubt God's hand in sending him to prison for such an ordeal. Again, he felt himself growing angry that God had left him in prison so long to languish and deteriorate in health. Now he would surely die, and who would care?

When he allowed himself to think such thoughts, Chen could feel himself slipping back into depression. He was so miserable physically, mentally, and emotionally! During these dark moments, he sometimes thought he would just get off the train, lie down beside the tracks, and die.

But he knew he must not entertain these feelings! He had to think happy thoughts, to quote Scripture again, to sing the words to some simple song of salvation that would lift his spirits! He could not give up! He would not give in to Satan's temptations of doubt! He refused to drown in the waters of despair washing over him, and whenever he decided to praise God, something in his heart would always bring him back up for spiritual air! Unless God gave him permission to die, Chen still had work to do for the church!

137

"God is good!" Chen would repeat over and over again. More than anything, the promises in Scripture gave him comfort and lifted his spirits again and again. "All things work together for good to those who love God," he kept repeating to himself as the train slowly rumbled on toward the station in Lishui.

And God was good. Chen did live to see his family again. Painful as it was to sit on those hard benches, he made the trip with no fainting spells, though he did have some serious spasms of coughing that brought up fresh blood. Fortunately, his parents were there to meet him at the train station, since Chow had notified them in a letter that he would be coming. Chen's family was shocked at his appearance, of course, and his mother wept uncontrollably when she saw his condition. To them, he was the picture of walking death, but like his church family in Wu Xi, they were glad he had lived long enough to see them once again.

Chapter 32

The trip home from the train station was again a real ordeal, since they had to take him on a handcart a neighbor had lent them. Every minute of the bouncing cart ride on the bumpy streets was agonizingly painful.

Visitors were called in to have a special prayer meeting that evening. Many wanted to know the details of his imprisonment, but Chen spent his time instead sharing the Bible promises that had kept him strong. Everyone was blessed by his moving testimony, and they all praised God for bringing Chen home alive.

It was amazing to them that Chen could be so upbeat, since his appearance told a different story. By now, he was coughing up too much blood, and he could see the anxiety in the eyes of friends and family. Fearful that he might die at any time, they took him to see the doctor the next day.

When they arrived at the clinic and the nurses put him on a scale, he weighed only fifty-five kilos, a mere shadow of his former self. As a grown man, he had never tipped the scales at less than eighty-five kilos. The doctor diagnosed Chen with anemia and a serious pulmonary disease, common health problems in China at this time because of the great famine sweeping the land.

However, to everyone's surprise, he gave Chen a fairly simple treatment plan. "Good food, vitamins, and plenty of rest will help more than anything," he told Chen and his family. "The going will be touch and go, but we must hope for the best, and time will make up the difference."

But Chen's family knew his journey to health would probably not be so easy. He needed medical care, and fast. He was still coughing up blood, and lots of it. They must get him serious help! There was no time to waste!

But Chen assured them that God was in control. "He will give me the strength to live another day. How can I continue to serve in God's vineyard if I die?"

When a neighbor came to visit and saw Chen's condition, he urged him to visit a special hospital for treating lung diseases in a city not far away. "The trip will be hard for you, but I think it is the only way," he said. "My sister had a condition like yours, and this was the one thing that helped."

Chen dreaded another painful trip but agreed to go. If what the neighbor said was true, there were no other options. He must make the journey.

Again, the trip was long and painful, but when he arrived at the hospital, he sensed that here he could get good medical treatment. God had indeed brought him to this hospital to be nursed back to health. Amazingly, there were only two patients assigned to each hospital room. When comparing this situation to his previous year in prison, he almost had to laugh. First, he'd had over forty cellmates, then eight, and now only two.

There were thirty patients with conditions much like his own in the lung ward, and immediately he realized God had once again set him up for evangelism. He was glad for the privacy of his new hospital room, but he knew he would never be able to keep to himself, even if he did need the rest to get better. *"Hardships and misfortune are never an excuse for avoiding our duty to witness for God,"* he remembered hearing his father say many times.

All that first day in the hospital when Chen wasn't coughing or vomiting blood, he was planning how he would introduce his new roommate to God. Chen was weak from the anemia that plagued his body, but if nothing else, he could always share the love of Jesus from his hospital bed.

That evening, Chen shared the gospel story with Fai, his roommate. "For God so loved the world that He gave His only begotten Son," Chen told him, "that whoever believes in Him should not perish but have everlasting life" (John 3:16, NKJV).

As the days passed in the hospital, Chen began to feel much better. The new diet he was given really helped, and he could feel life returning to his body once again. Soon he was on his feet getting around to visit all the patients in his ward so he could talk to them about the love of Jesus. Many had never heard such things, and Chen's words of hope inspired them. That the God of heaven loved and cared for them was wonderful news.

On his rounds through the ward one day, Chen stopped to encourage Meizhen, a young woman with the same lung disease he had. She had arrived just the day before and was spitting up almost as much blood as he was. Chen learned that Meizhen had been attending a local university and was all alone without the support of her family when she got sick. There was no one to visit her in the hospital. To cheer her heart, he prayed with her and quoted comforting passages of Scripture.

"God is our refuge and strength, a very present help in trouble," Chen said (Psalm 46:1, NKJV). "Sometimes He helps us right away. Sometimes He makes us wait, but always He helps us when we need Him most. We might not always be patient enough to believe that, but God never makes mistakes."

"Your God would help me?" Meizhen looked puzzled, thinking of all the gods she had heard of in the Chinese culture. "He's not my God. I don't know anything about Him. Why would He do this for me?"

"Because He loves you with an everlasting love," Chen said confidently. "It's that simple. God says, 'With lovingkindness I have drawn you' [Jeremiah 31:3, NKJV]. You are a daughter of the living God, Meizhen. He made you in His image. That's why He loves you."

Meizhen looked troubled. "I have never heard such things, but I don't suppose it matters much. Right now I'm very sick, and I'm afraid to die. That's all I can think about."

"I understand how you feel. I've been sick for a long time myself, but God has been with me helping me survive." Chen sat down beside Meizhen's bed. "Trust me. When you know God, you don't have to be afraid. When we walk through the valley of the shadow of death, He will be with us [see Psalm 23:4]. God has promised us that we can cast all our cares on Him. He will never forsake us even in death."

"Really, now. This is all true?" Meizhen stared at Chen as though a new door to the future had opened for her. And in all honesty, it had. "How do you do it?" she asked, a light of hope now shining from her eyes. "How do you keep your spirits up knowing you've been so sick you could die?"

"It is my belief in Jesus and His love for me," he told her. "That's the difference. When I think of all God has blessed me with, it's hard to feel down. I can walk, I can see, I'm alive, and I owe it all to Jesus."

In the days that followed, Chen came back often to talk with Meizhen about God. He showed her how the Bible could be good medicine to relieve her worries about her illness. He told her how he had used verses of Scripture to comfort himself when he was in prison, when he was suffering through the long months of mind-numbing interrogations, and when the prison officers had tried to starve him into submission.

Meizhen was clearly impressed with Chen's positive attitude and strong faith in God. His words of encouragement convinced her that Jesus cared about her very much even though she wasn't yet a Christian. More important, she came to realize that Jesus had died for her sins, and because of this, she could have eternal life.

Not surprisingly, by the time Meizhen regained her health, she had come to love Chen's God and the great truths of the Bible as taught by Seventh-day Adventist Christians. She had learned to trust in the promises of God's Word, and Chen had even helped her memorize some special verses of Scripture.

When the doctors told Meizhen she was well enough to leave the hospital, she was ecstatic! "Now I can go back home and make a full recovery," she said excitedly when she told Chen the news. "My hometown of Yulin in the Shanxi Province has beautiful mountains, and the doctor says the climate is good for people who suffer from lung diseases! God has saved my life!" she added, her face all aglow. "He has given me back my health! I can never thank you enough, Chen, for introducing me to Jesus! How can I ever repay you?"

Chains in China

Chapter 33

D on't thank me," Chen grinned from ear to ear. "Jesus made you well. I just pointed you to Him, the Great Physician."

"Well then, thank you for pointing me to Jesus!" she bubbled excitedly. "Hey! Listen! I have a great idea! Why don't you come with me to my village? You'll love it there! The climate is dry and the air is fresh with no pollution. You can invite your roommate along too, if you want. I'm sure you would both recover quickly there."

The two men were given clearance by their doctors and gladly accepted Meizhen's invitation to visit her mountain valley home. It was an offer they couldn't refuse. After writing a letter to their families telling them about their recovery and the trip to the mountains, they all started off together. Chen had no money, but Meizhen offered to pay his way. "It's the least I can do to thank you for introducing me to Jesus!" she said with shining eyes.

And so they made the trip. For Meizhen, it was a dream come true. She was going home to live. She had survived a fatal disease and inherited eternal life in the process. For Chen, it was the beginning of a new chapter too. The road ahead was about to take another turn, and life for him would never be the same again.

Life with Meizhen's family in the village of Yulin was everything Chen had hoped it would be. They were simple, unhurried, and very friendly. He fit right in, and her family liked him immediately.

The villagers were also excited about his arrival. He was a visitor from the big city, and that was a real plus for them. People from the big cities never came this way. By now, Chen was in his early thirties, and to all the young men in town, he seemed sophisticated, a man with connections to an outside world they would never see. To the older men of the village, he was simply Brother Chen.

Nights around the warm evening fires now became a real treat for everyone. Chen, of course, was the celebrity, and they wanted to hear all he had to say. Wisely, he spent the time sharing the great truths of the Bible, the life-changing stories within its pages, and tales of his adventures for Jesus.

He was a gifted speaker, and before long, Meizhen's family was ready to accept him as if he had always been one of them. None of the villagers were Christian, but that was not a problem for Chen. Once again, he realized God had placed him exactly where he needed to be for a very special task. His job now was to win Meizhen's family to Jesus.

Chen's roommate from the hospital decided he couldn't stand the quiet life of the mountain village and soon left. Chen, however, gladly stayed on. The cool mountain air was like a tonic for his lung problems, and before very long, he was feeling much better.

Meizhen and Chen continued studying the Bible together every day, and with every Bible lesson they discussed, she grew closer to God. "How could I have thought I was really living before I met Jesus?" she asked Chen one day. "In my old life, I was always thinking about having a good time. I did not think about death because I was young and alive! But my sickness changed all that. Now Jesus is my life! I think of Him all day long, and in Him I have the hope of eternal life. Now I am not afraid of death."

And, for Chen of course, spending so much time with Meizhen began to have an impact on their relationship too. Besides studying the Bible together, they spent many hours working together in the little garden behind Meizhen's house. Sometimes they tried their hand at cooking Chinese dishes; other times they went hiking in the mountains together. To Meizhen, Chen was clearly becoming more than just a friend.

Her interest in him continued to grow, but he never seemed to notice, or if he did, he simply figured she was experiencing big brother syndrome. After all, he was quite a bit older than she was.

But Meizhen would have none of his nonsense. In fact, she became rather bold about her feelings for Chen. *Someone has to do something about it,* she reasoned. *If I don't, who will?*

One day, while they were walking on a mountain trail, she asked him outright if he loved her. "I want to marry you," she said boldly.

"You must be joking," he laughed, plucking a twig to chew on from a nearby branch.

"Women don't joke about such things," she countered.

He tried to shrug off what he supposed was just an infatuation for him. "You're young and naïve. What do you know about love and marriage?" he reasoned, but she would not be dissuaded.

"This is serious business," she announced. "You need a woman to take care of you, and I need a husband in my life."

"Oh, come now," he protested, stopping to face her on the sun-dappled trail, "must I remind you that I'm an ex-convict?"

"Doesn't matter!" she argued. "I know the whole story."

"And your brother is a Chinese military officer. That family combination would never be tolerated by the government, considering I spent time in prison."

But still she persisted. "I'm not going away just because you are afraid to admit the truth. It's obvious. We belong together. Anyone can see that."

Then he told her of his failure and disappointment with his previous marriage, but she swept aside these explanations too. "Your previous wife left you because you were a Seventh-day Adventist Christian. She did not want to live life with a man who would put God before her. I do," she told him with admiring eyes. "I see that you are a man of God, and that to me makes all the difference in the world."

Chen took Meizhen's hand and sat her down beside him on a log along the trail. "I don't think you fully understand what you are getting yourself into," he began, "but let me try to explain. If we were ever to be married, you would have to become a baptized Seventh-day Adventist Christian. You would have to be willing to sacrifice the comforts of life and become poor. You would have to be willing to be a missionary, travel from place to place, and suffer a life of persecution, maybe even death. That's how it is in the life of a Christian," he told her, his eyes intent with the message he felt she did not comprehend. "The devil will see to that! Look what he has put me through already!"

Meizhen stared right back at Chen, as if his words were going right through her. "And you think these are obstacles for me?" she asked incredulously. "Have you forgotten that before I even knew you I was targeted by Satan? Before I met you and heard the story of salvation, I was scheduled to die. You were the one who brought me the good news of life and prayed for me. You were the one who told me to never give up and to live a life of faith that can move mountains. And so I have moved mountains. My dreaded lung disease is a perfect example. Now the only mountain I have to move is you, and if I can do that, it will be a real miracle!"

Chapter 34

Chen and Meizhen laughed so hard they nearly fell off the log, making two little finches sitting on a nearby branch fly away in surprise.

When they finally stopped laughing, Meizhen took Chen's big hands in her tiny ones. "I want to share your life," she said quietly. "Your bitter life will be mine, your people my people. We have the same ideas about sharing the gospel story and going to heaven, and that is what's most important."

Chen could no longer protest, and so they set the wedding date. "What good will it do to argue with a woman as stubborn as you?" he grinned.

But there was no one to marry them. The Chinese communist government did not provide for wedding celebrations in those days. All the churches had been shut down, and no one knew where they might find a Christian pastor. No one wanted to attract unwanted attention and upset the government officials, so Chen and Meizhen conducted a simple wedding ceremony with family where they could exchange vows.

Months passed like birds on the wing, and the couple was very happy together. In the second year of their marriage, Meizhen gave birth to Ping, a baby boy. Everyone was happy for Chen and Meizhen, especially her mother. So much had changed for Meizhen. She had left home just two years before with a fatal lung disease, never to return. Now she was married to a wonderful man and had given birth to a little baby, the greatest miracle of life!

However, this new joy was not to last. When the baby was just eighteen days old, Meizhen felt a stabbing pain in her chest. She could not breathe well, and the doctor's prescribed medicine didn't help. Terrified of the outcome, Chen rushed her off to a local hospital.

Meizhen was treated immediately, but her diagnosis was not good. After her physician, Dr. Fuhua, had stabilized her and examined her thoroughly, he took Chen aside and gave him the worst news possible. "Your wife is resting now, Chen, but her situation is very serious. She is experiencing acute cardiac failure, a complication due to the pulmonary disease she has been suffering from for so long."

"Cardiac failure! That's not possible!" Chen couldn't believe his ears. "She's just a young woman, only twenty-three years old!"

"I'm as surprised as you are about this sudden setback," Dr. Fuhua said slowly. "This would never have happened if it hadn't been for the disease. She has regained much of her strength after the long illness, but the damage done to her heart has been too much for her. And unfortunately, the pregnancy put a strain on her too."

Chen fell back into a chair. "There must be a way to save her!" he said in desperation. "We can't just let her die! God needs us as His witnesses here in Yulin. Oh Lord, please don't let her die!" he moaned.

The doctor came to stand by Chen's side. "You did all the right things, Chen, but there's nothing we can do for her," he said sadly. "Even God cannot help her. The damage in her heart is just too great."

"How can this have happened?" Chen covered his face with his hands. "She has made so much progress! We thought the mountain air would be the very thing she needed." He glanced up at Dr. Fuhua hopefully. "Can't you do something for her?" he pleaded. "You're a doctor!"

The doctor paused, trying to think of the right words to say. "Meizhen has only days to live, a week or two at best. She is a tough girl, and her body is fighting bravely to hang on, but it's just a matter of time now. Her death is inevitable."

Chen fell silent, his energy gone, his spirit crushed. *She is such a cheerful person!* he thought, tears coming to his eyes. *She never complains about anything in life. She knows how to live simply and has sacrificed so much to be a pastor's wife.*

Suddenly, he remembered their baby. "The baby!" Chen glanced up at the doctor. "How can I care for my son and still provide for the family?"

"How about her mother?" the doctor offered. "Can she help? Or maybe sisters. Does Meizhen have sisters?" The doctor seemed unusually kind, more compassionate than Chen would have expected from a medical man working for the Chinese government.

"Her mother is older, and she has no sisters," Chen admitted, his face the picture of sadness.

"I must go and tend to my other patients," the doctor finally said, "but I'll be back later if you need me."

For the longest time, Chen could do nothing. He just sat there in the waiting room of the hospital, unaware of his surroundings, it seemed. Evening approached, but he hardly noticed the passing of time. Finally, the doctor returned with a clipboard in his hand.

"I am going to ask you to read this form, and when you are ready, please sign it," the doctor said.

Chains in China

Chen stared at the doctor, only vaguely hearing his words. "What is the reason for this form?" he mumbled.

"Meizhen's strength is waning," the doctor said. "This form states that she is critically ill, and that the hospital is relieved from all responsibility regarding her health and recovery."

The doctor's words hit Chen like a ton of bricks. "No! I will not sign it!" he stammered, rallying himself for the moment. "She's not going to die! I won't let her. You can't let her die. She must live!"

"There is nothing more we can do for her." The doctor looked weary. "Please sign the form."

Chen took the pen and held it in his hand for the longest time. The tears couldn't be stopped now, and he could hardly see to sign his name. It seemed life for him was coming to an end, just as it was for Meizhen.

"Now, go be with Meizhen," the doctor urged. "Spend her final hours with her."

Chen went into Meizhen's room and stood looking down at her. By now, she was unconscious and was having a hard time breathing. It was heartbreaking to see her suffering in such a condition, but there were other things to think about now. Losing Meizhen would be devastating for her family, and, of course, the baby. Their little baby would grow up never knowing the lovely young mother Meizhen had become.

But in his heart, Chen knew he would miss her the most. In their short time together, she had become the absolute joy of his life. Such a wonderful package of happiness and energy and love! How could he continue on without her? He had suffered so much for the sake of Jesus! God had guided him through every evangelistic adventure, every trial that had tested his zeal for the Sabbath, every setback in his first marriage. The angels had preserved Chen all those months in the prison of death, but it seemed now that Meizhen's death would be his greatest tragedy yet.

Chen fell on his knees beside her bed and prayed as he had never prayed before. The light of his life was about to go out, and there was nothing he could do to stop it.

Hours passed, but Chen hardly noticed. Nurses came and went on their rounds of duty. The whirring of an electric fan purred softly, rustling the curtains on the hospital window. Somewhere outside, evening crickets tried to lift his spirits with their incessant chirping, but Chen was oblivious. All he knew was that his precious wife was dying, and the doctors could not save her. It was just a matter of time now, and she would be gone.

Chapter 35

He had grown so attached to this wonderful woman in the short time they had been together. How could he live without her? Would God let the love of his life be torn from his side? Even now, as she lay unconscious, she was the picture of beauty and perfect loveliness.

And the baby? How could he raise Ping without a mother? A baby needed the love and care of a mother. For Chen and his little son, things looked bleak indeed. Without Meizhen's companionship, life would never be the same, and the baby now would have to grow up without a mother.

As the reality of Meizhen's plight set in, Chen began to grow more and more despondent. He could feel himself being sucked down into a pit of despair. It was a terrible feeling! He could not see his way through the fog of pain threatening to swallow him up. The forces of evil crowded their way in and threatened to blot out his faith in God. Worse yet, he seemed helpless to do anything about it.

"Please Lord," Chen begged, "You are my only hope! I feel as if the light of heaven is being extinguished from my heart. You must save Meizhen! Unless You do something miraculous, Lord, she will die. Please save her! Please heal my Meizhen and bring her back to me. You are the Great Physician, the Healer of all diseases. Help us Lord, and help my unbelief!" he added.

Chen's frantic pleadings were fired with desperation, and he felt himself growing impatient with God. And yet he could not find relief. The more he prayed, the farther he seemed from God. "Why will You not hear my prayers?" he cried out in frustration and anger.

And then his mind went back to the long months in prison, to the endless days and nights of torture and misery. God had been with him and preserved him at that time. He had been gracious to Chen, giving him hope when he needed it, and peace and comfort in his heart when it mattered most. God had been his secret place and his overarching shadow of protection from the evil one. The Lord had been his refuge and strength to withstand despair, depression, and deadly diseases.

Your people have always been able to call on the Lord in their trouble, Chen prayed. *When we need You most, You always save us in times of distress* [see Psalm 107:13]. *It is good for me to draw near to You, Lord. I know I can put my trust in the Lord God of my fathers* [see Psalm 73:28]. Chen's mind was in a whirl. More than anything, he wanted to keep his hold on God. *I must trust You at all times, Lord,* he continued in prayer as he remembered favorite verses of Scripture. *I pour out my heart before You, because You are my refuge* [see Psalm 62:8].

Slowly but surely, the calm of heaven began to settle upon Chen. He could feel the power of holy angels pushing back the evil that surrounded him and Meizhen where she lay on her bed. Peace filled his heart. The Spirit of God had returned, and Chen's tired shoulders began to relax. God was in this place, and that was all that mattered. Whatever God chose to do for Meizhen would be fine with Chen. "God's ways are always best," he whispered as he bowed in submission to the will of the Father.

The darkness of night began to lift as dawn melted the eastern skies. Gone was the blackness of despair that had covered Chen like a shroud. Gone were the questions he had raised in his mind about the goodness of God. The doctor and a new shift of nurses would soon be arriving at the hospital, but it would be a different Chen greeting them. He had prayed through the night, and by faith, he had come away the victor.

Suddenly, Chen felt the bed move, and he opened his eyes to see Meizhen looking at him. "Thank you for staying with me," she smiled, and Chen thought he had never seen a more beautiful face in the world.

"You're awake!" Chen caught his breath. "You're alive!" He clutched at her but remained on his knees by her bed. "Thank God! Thank God!" he repeated over and over again as he buried his face in the bed sheet. "You're alive! You're alive! Thank You, Jesus, for bringing Meizhen back to me!"

"Why are you crying?" Meizhen seemed unaware of the battle that had been raging for her life, but she sensed now that something big had taken place.

"You have been very sick, my dear. It's your heart." Chen choked back tears of happiness. "How do you feel?"

"I feel good. Quite good, actually. Better than I have felt in a long, long time." Her eyes showed her confusion. "It was that bad?"

"We almost lost you." Chen took a deep breath to bring himself back to reality. "The doctors said you only had days to live and that I should prepare for your death. It was the worst night of my life!"

Meizhen reached out and took Chen's hand. "Well, I'm not dead, and I'm not going to die. I feel fine. Praise God for His loving goodness and many mercies!"

"It's a miracle!" Chen kept repeating in wonder. "A miracle!" He bowed his head again. It frightened him to think that his faith in God's power had wavered, and that it might have cost Meizhen her life.

The commotion in Meizhen's room soon brought the nurses on duty in, and with them came exclamations of surprise and shock. "She's awake!" they began shouting and rushed out to call the doctors in. "Meizhen is awake! Meizhen's God has healed her and made her well again!"

Within seconds, it seemed, everyone had crowded into Meizhen's small room. Oohs and aahs filled the air as they asked Chen for details and explanations of how such a thing could be. Meizhen had experienced a miracle of the most amazing sort, and they were all witnesses to it!

"This is astonishing!" said Dr. Fuhua after he had examined Meizhen and done several tests on her heart. "In all my days as a doctor, I have never seen such a miraculous transformation for someone in Meizhen's condition. Her heart valves were already damaged, and she was quickly moving toward a state of cardiac arrest. I have no explanation for this incredible recovery! It defies all the explanations of modern medicine!"

A chorus of babbling filled the hospital room as nurses and doctors together continued their exclamations of wonder. But, suddenly, they were all interrupted by Meizhen's small voice.

"Jesus did this," she said softly. "My God shall supply all my needs in Christ Jesus." She smiled up at Chen and squeezed his hand. "My husband taught me that verse from the Bible. Jesus is the Healer of our minds and bodies, and He has made me well again. He is the Great Physician, and I must give credit to no one else. I think it must be a miracle He has done for me today."

Dr. Fuhua grew quiet, and a solemn expression came over his face. "Then your God is truly amazing!" he added. "I have no other explanation!"

And truly it was a miracle! Meizhen had made a full recovery. A few hours before, the doctors had been willing to write her off as good as dead, and they had wanted Chen to do the same. But now she had been given another chance on life.

The rest of the hospital staff came to give her a full examination, but they could find no symptoms of her recent heart condition. Even more surprising, they could also find no evidence of scarring in her heart valves or damage to her lungs or other organs.

When everyone had finally left Meizhen to tend to their regular hospital duties, Chen again dropped to his knees by her bedside. What could he say? How could he account for Meizhen's full recovery? The whole episode now seemed surreal in his mind—so bizarre and so very unexpected! And yet Chen knew it should not be a stretch of faith for him. He had prayed to the God of heaven to give Meizhen back her life, and that was exactly what God had done. Should this be so surprising when through all of Chen's life that was exactly what God had been doing—answering prayers and performing miracles?

Chen remained by Meizhen's bed on his knees in prayer, his face buried in the bed sheet. He knew his faith had been challenged in terms of his belief in the power of God to perform such miracles. He had been tested, but God had been good and had answered his prayers for his wife in spite of his lack of faith.

A lump grew in his throat, and a sense of shame began to build within him for his failure to trust God. He had not been fair with God in his prayers. He had not been fair in his expectations that Meizhen be healed. *God is not a vending machine,* he reminded himself. No matter the outcome for Meizhen, he knew beyond all doubt that God was her Refuge and Strength in good times and bad. Hadn't Chen's own grueling ordeal in the Wu Xi prison shown him that clearly?

That God might have Meizhen's best good in mind, whether for healing or not, was not a question in Chen's mind any longer. He was so overwhelmed by Meizhen's new lease on life, and his heartbeat quickened in praise for heaven's goodness. "All things work together for good to those who love God" (Romans 8:28, NKJV).

Epilogue

During the years that followed, Chen suffered much for the cause of Jesus, but never again in prison. The local government officials continued watching him, but because he was a man of integrity and had a reputation for kindness to those in need, they left him alone.

And God continued to bless Chen and Meizhen. Often Chen was called to minister to the sick and dying. Many were healed miraculously, and he always had a word of comfort for these invalids. Chen's reputation as a man of gifts spread throughout the area. People began to treat him with something akin to reverence and even awe. Here was a man among them who walked and talked with the God of heaven. Of course, Chen always pointed people to Jesus, reminding them it was the power of God in their lives that could heal them and rescue them from sin.

Before long, he started a small Adventist church group in Meizhen's hometown; in this way, he won many converts to Jesus. As always, Chen and Meizhen enjoyed sharing the gospel, and everywhere they went they told the story of how God had spared their lives miraculously.

Sometimes Chen was called on to speak at public meetings or gatherings at holiday events. Sometimes he was asked to share the stories of his travels, and when the town leaders in Yulin discovered he was an exceptional writer, they hired him to do some specialized calligraphy for the government on the walls of buildings in public places. This gave Chen a way of supporting his family while he continued to lead his church group.

And then in 1976, Chairman Mao Zedong died, and Deng Xiaoping later took the reins of government. Deng Xiaoping did not promote the philosophy of Chairman Mao and as a result was much more tolerant of the traditional religions in China. Thankfully, from that day forward, circumstances began to change for Christian churches in China little by little. Within a few short years, Adventist churches were opening up everywhere, and the gospel began to make strides in a land where Mao Zedong had once tried to stamp out Christianity.

By 1979, Pastor Chen had returned to his own hometown to reopen the church for worship. His congregation of worshipers prospered and grew large quickly, and soon they had to split into smaller groups.

By now, Chen had become famous as a speaker and proved to be a blessing to Seventh-day Adventists everywhere. Non-Seventh-day Adventist churches heard about Pastor Chen's story of faithfulness and his zeal for the gospel, and soon they were inviting him to share the good news of the three angels' messages in their churches.

As of this writing, Pastor Chen is in his late eighties and lives in eastern China with his wife, Meizhen. They continue to witness for Jesus in their community and look for the soon coming of Jesus, who died for them that they might have eternal life. Chen's testimony for Jesus has always been the most important task for him as a Christian. The theme for his life is found in Psalm 1:1–3:

Blessed is the man
Who walks not in the counsel of the ungodly,
Nor stands in the path of sinners,
Nor sits in the seat of the scornful;
But his delight is in the law of the LORD,
And in His law he meditates day and night.
He shall be like a tree
Planted by the rivers of water,
That brings forth its fruit in its season,
Whose leaf also shall not wither,
And whatever he does shall prosper (NKJV).

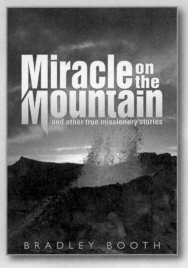
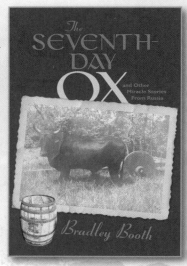
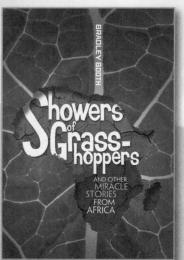